Religion and Violence

ATF Press
Adelaide

Religion and Violence

Edited by

Jonathan Inkpin

ATF Press
Adelaide

Contents

Editorial

'Do not think that I have come to bring peace to the earth; I have not come to bring peace but a sword.' (Matthew 10:42)

'Blessed are the peacemakers, for they will be called children of God.'
(Matthew 5:9)

At the heart of the Christian faith is an engagement with violence. The cross itself is the pre-eminent site of struggle—human, earthly, cosmic and divine. Today that cross is seen in a multiplicity of sites of violence, public and private, at home and overseas. This in itself would demand theological attention. The religious challenge is however much deeper. Whether considered in the light of the Middle East, Bosnia, the Sudan, Ireland, or, closer to home in Australia, South-East Asia, religion itself appears as hugely problematic. At the very least, judged by its fruits, it is highly paradoxical. Is the sword of the spirit a means of liberation from human, material and spiritual oppression, or is it a particularly insidious instrument of destruction?

For contemporary Australians still reeling from the impact of the Bali bombings and the industry of global terrorism, the religious dimensions of violence have in recent times undoubtedly broken in as a painfully rude shock. This is especially the case for those who have prided themselves in the allegedly 'secular' nature of Australian society, and for those whose view of religion is of a comfortable optional accoutrement to the search for the perfect 'lifestyle' in the 'lucky country'. Religion, at its cruel braying worst and its awe-inspiring challenging best, has forced itself back on the agenda. It is, at the very least, a fractious element to be managed at home and a potent factor to navigate overseas.

Is religion responsible for violence? In what ways do religious commitments themselves contribute to violence? Is it possible to find a way through to peace and reconciliation? The following essays seek to address these questions. They represent a range of different voices, drawing on Asian, European, and Pacific, as well as specifically Australian, experiences. They speak out of practical encounter as well as academic rigour.

At the core of the theological challenge in addressing violence is the review of the way in which religious faith is constructed and conveyed. The

first essay in this collection, by Patrick McInerney, thus considers the important methodological contributions made by scholars such as Girard and
Lonergan, not least in relation to the development and meaning of key
Christian doctrines such as that of the atonement, heavily laden as this has
been with conceptions of blood and sacrifice. Re-examining our religious
traditions and rediscovering their liberating potential is similarly at the heart
of James Haire's intercultural approach to building communities of peace.
Drawing on his own personal stories of encountering violence, he outlines the
Pauline understanding of community and its eschatological peacemaking
potential, articulating how the expression of religion in and across different
cultural milieux can contribute to violence or build peace.

Such reflections do not take place in a vacuum but are themselves a
product of our times and worldwide context. The question of how we live with
difference is central. Here, as Kathy Galloway reflects, the experience of the
marginalised challenges us to 'journey from assimilation through multiculturalism to solidarity with the poorest and most vulnerable'. Women's
experience, in life and bible story, is a powerful window into how we can
maintain structures of racism and injustice or 'witness to a different way of
being'.

Such voices all give grounds for hope that a 'global ethic' might be
possible. Do such initiatives as the World Council of Churches' 'Decade to
Overcome Violence: Churches Seeking Peace and Reconciliation' provide
such a framework? Acknowledging the wide variety of interests at stake, what
are the theological sticking points in the evolution of such a worldview? My
own contribution to this volume seeks to tease out some of these issues in the
current ecumenical journey and to highlight the importance of the widely
shared religious concepts of truth, justice, mercy-power and community
(*koinonia*) for establishing a common platform for the transfiguration of
violence.

A persistent theme is the need to embody our relationship to violence, by
fully recognising and touching the other, and connecting to our own impulses
and search for violence and exclusivity. Theology which truly addresses our
painful tendency to violence is thus, as Kathy Galloway reminds us, what
Kosuke Koyama called a 'see, hear, touch' gospel. The final two essays here
seek to express this in the context of Indonesian and Pacific Islander images
and experiences. From a Muslim perspective, Mohammad Iqbal Ahnaf
explores how key Islamic principles, such as that of *Islah* (peace settlement),
can help in the journey of reconciliation with justice in Indonesia. How is
truth to be heard and justice done with adequate reparation in crimes

perpetrated by an authoritarian regime? Is it possible to reach a satisfactory resolution through religious methods when secular institutions have been compromised?

Perhaps we can look towards reconciliation only when we are prepared to face the many different bodies which shape our lives and give power to religious violence or its transformation: among them sacred texts, interpreters, power, status, gender, security, ritual, and those 'other' than ourselves. In his beautiful, yet poignant, essay Jione Havea thus concludes this collection by tracing a physiognomy of violence, outlining an approach of religious sensibility which, in offering a way out, properly acknowledges both the pleasure and the grief found in violence. The answer, he suggests, in common with his fellow essayists, is not found by simply attempting to reject violence. Rather, we need to gather on the mat together and hear the voices of others, 'crying out, "Wait. Sit. Talk to us first!"'.

Jonathan Inkpin

1

Religion and Violence

Patrick J McInerney

Introduction

I can still remember clearly the exact time and place. It was the afternoon of the 13 September 2001. I was driving to a lecture and listening to talk-back radio, the airwaves full of fascinated revulsion at the traumatic events in New York, Washington and Pennsylvania two days earlier.[1] The caller proclaimed triumphantly: 'See! Religion is the problem! Get rid of religion, and you will get rid of the violence!'

These few words, in all their simplicity, starkness and seeming credibility, capture the popular myth that religion is deeply complicit in violence.

Evidence for the popular myth

The most common evidence presented in support of the case are:

- the Crusades, the series of military adventurism by Christian European powers against the Muslim rule in the Holy Land in the eleventh to the thirteenth century;
- the Inquisition unleashed by Catholic authorities for the suppression of so-called heretics in the thirteenth century;
- the Wars of Religion between Catholics and Protestants that divided sixteenth and seventeenth century Europe;
- the colonisation of much of the world by European 'Christian' empires from the sixteenth century onwards.[2]

---

1. For an interpretation of this phenomenon see James Alison, *On Being Liked* (London: Darton, Longman & Todd, 2003), 3–8.
2. The above are all examples from 'Christian' and European history, but to them could be added the violence done in Islam's initial expansion into previously Christian-majority territories, and between different Islamic empires, the eruptions of communal violence between Hindu and Muslim and Sikh in the sub-continent, the dispossession of the Palestinians by the State of Israel, the ethnic violence in

If such evidence is considered dated, contemporary indicators are the religious extremists who perpetrate terrorist acts of suicide-murder against civilian populations. The most infamous of these recent events was the death of over 3,000 people in the attacks against 'iconic' US buildings on 11 September 2001 to which the above-mentioned caller was referring.[3] Since then there have been the Bali nightclub bombings on 12 October 2002 in which 202 people died (including eighty-eight Australians) and 209 were injured; the Madrid train bombings on 11 March 2004, killing 191 and wounding 2,050; the school siege in Beslan from the 1–3 September 2004 in which 331 died, more than half of them children, and 700 were injured; and the London transport bombings on 7 July 2005 in which fifty-two commuters died and 700 others were injured. The bloody litany of 'religiously-associated'—if not 'religiously-motivated'—violence continues in Afghanistan, in Iraq, in the Palestinian Territories, and in Sudan.[4]

Evidence against the popular myth

However, despite this seemingly overwhelming indictment of religion, its accusers overlook the fact that the greatest mass murderers of the twentieth century had little or nothing to do with religion:

- Stalin's regime (1924–53) resulted in twenty million deaths;[5]
- Hitler's Nazi regime and the European war led to forty-two million deaths, including the industrial execution of some six million Jews in the *Shoah*;

---

predominantly Buddhist Sri Lanka and Cambodia—and many others. For all these examples one could argue, and for the most part argue rightly, that violence was the exception to the rule, but even that admission confirms that violence has been a part of the history of religious believers.

3. 'Iconic', because representing economic wealth, military might, and (possibly) political power.
4. To counter the stereotypes and oversimplifications that propagandists against religion readily overlook, I feel obliged to state clearly that the extremists involved in the above-named incidents are a very tiny fringe minority who act ostensibly in the name of their religion but in violation of its cardinal principles, and they certainly do not represent the vast majority of their co-religionists who are appalled at that behaviour and at the distortion of their religion that it involves.
5. Statistics from <http://users.erols.com/mwhite28/warstat1.htm >.

- Mao Zedong's regime (1949–75) led to forty (or seventy-seven) million deaths.[6]

However, these 'secular' examples do not completely exonerate religion, for although the perpetrators of these massive crimes against humanity used ethnic and nationalist ideals to promote their political ends, it can be said that they did so with deadly *religious* fervour.

Moreover, in the face of such immense atrocities, the accusations and counter-accusations of whether religionists or atheists killed more sound very petty, much like the childish taunts sometime heard in playgrounds of 'my daddy's house/car/salary is bigger/better/faster than your daddy's!'

In rebuttal of the popular myth, it must be said that when religion is weighed in the balance, the scales are not wholly tilted towards violence. Throughout history, religion has inspired, and continues to inspire, self-sacrifice and dedication in working for non-violence, peace, justice, and reconciliation. Although the conservatism of religious believers has at times led them to oppose innovations in health, education, social welfare, economics, politics, ethics, liberation struggles, and environmental issues, more often than not they have been initiators and motivators in these areas of service to the common good, responding to the challenges and initiatives of others, and providing many personnel for grassroots involvement and leadership of these tasks.

In defence of religion, believers rightly claim that it is only when the complete dedication and devotion that religion inspires is *used, abused,* and *misused* for ulterior ends that religion contributes to violence. In these instances, the underlying issue is not religion. It is usually economic, ethnic, social, or political, but religion has willingly or unwillingly been co-opted to those ends.

Despite the validity of these rebuttals, they are somewhat disingenuous and not wholly convincing. Religious texts—like the Bible, the *Qur'an* and the *Bhagavad Gita*—have so many accounts of God or gods taking part in battles and wars that religion cannot escape the accusation that it is compromised by violence. All too often in history, religious believers have succumbed to committing or condoning violence under the banner cry of *Deus*

---

6. The higher figure: <http://www.prisonplanet.com/articles/november2005/29110 5morelethal.htm >.

Veult.[7] The co-incidence of religion and violence throughout history is too consistent and too pervasive to exonerate religion completely.

The possibility of a scientific account

Is it possible to go beyond the claims and counterclaims with regard to the popular myth? Is it possible to make a more scientific evaluation? Such a task involves analysis of all religions throughout all of human history and is beyond the scope of a paper such as this, but I will offer two contributions to that larger task.

The first is to indicate the significance and relevance of the mimetic theory developed by the French intellectual René Girard. The other is to apply one of the schemata of Canadian philosopher-theologian, Bernard Lonergan, to current world process. My conclusion will be that the conjunction of these two ideas provides a framework for understanding the 'religiously-inspired' violence that seems prevalent in our day.

Mimetic theory

Through reflection on literature René Girard has developed what he calls mimetic theory. It is an analysis of the role that desire and violence play in cultural origins.[8]

Very briefly, 'we desire according to the desire of another'.[9] Desire in itself is a good thing, and necessary for human becoming. But precisely because our desire is awakened and modelled by an other, inevitably we become rivals of that other in our attempts to achieve the object of our

---

7. Literally: 'God wills it'. This is the cry with which the people hailed Pope Urban II's call for the First Crusade.
8. For a summary of the theory see James G Williams, 'Foreword', in *I See Satan Fall Like Lightning* (New York: Crossroad, 2001). Also 'A Bird's Eye View of Mimetic Theory', in James Alison, *Raising Abel: The Recovery of Eschatological Imagination* (New York: Crossroad Publishing Company 1996), 18–25. And 'René Girard's Mimetic Theory', in James Alison, *The Joy of Being Wrong: Original Sin Through Easter Eyes* (New York: Crossroad Publishing Company, 1998), 7–21. For a developed account see Michael Kirwan, *Discovering Girard* (London: Darton, Longman & Todd, 2004), according to James Alison, *Undergoing God: Dispatches from the Scene of a Break-In* (New York, London: Continuum, 2006), 50.
9. Alison, *On Being Liked*, 2.

common desire, and we define ourselves 'over against' that other.[10] When that desire is not met, either because the imitator cannot wrest the desired object from the original model, or because the competing rivalries prevent both of them from attaining it, the conflicting tension escalates and the frustrated desire mounts to exploding point.[11] The rivals face a crisis.

To prevent the explosion that threatens them, rather than acknowledging its source in their conflicted desires, the rivals conspire to find a victim, someone vulnerable, an outsider, a marginal figure, who can be blamed for the intolerable frustration and tension that they experience.[12] The former rivals then all unite against the victim—it is 'unanimity minus one'[13]—precisely in order to save society from destruction (or so they convince themselves).

All the conflicts and frustrations of society are projected onto the victim. In a paroxysm of accusation and self-righteousness, the rivals-become-co-conspirators expel the victim from society, quite often literally murdering him/her. 'Sacrifice and scapegoating are two different expressions of the same reality, the victim mechanism.'[14] In biblical terms, the victim is the scapegoat, the one who bears the sins of the nation (see Lev 11–16).

By the catharsis of expelling/killing the victim, the impending disaster is averted and society is saved. In contrast to the previous explosive rivalry and fractious tension and its violent resolution, there is now a lull after the storm. The perpetrators experience relief, peace, harmony, reconciliation. By an inversion of the earlier 'transferring blame' onto the victim, there is now a 'transferring of credit' onto the victim.[15] The one who was accused of being the cause of strife is now hailed as the cause of peace, and therefore must be a being of a higher order. 'This is the birth of the gods.'[16] The victim is thus 'sacralised', made holy, made the source of peace, the one who has united the community.

---

10. This is the basis of the rivalries and the conflicting dualities that beset society: Jew and Greek, slave and free, male and female (see also Gal 3:28).

11. Williams, 'Foreword', xi.

12. For an account of the institution of the scapegoat see Gil Bailie, *Violence Unveiled: Humanity at the Crossroads* (New York: Crossroad, 1995), 149–52.

13. Bailie, *Violence Unveiled*, 50. The author states that this is 'a phrase René Girard uses to describe the cathartic moment of scapegoating violence'.

14. Williams, 'Foreword', xv.

15. Williams, 'Foreword', xvi.

16. Williams, 'Foreword', xvi.

However, the foundation of that peace, the expulsion/murder that is its base, is covered up and disguised. This is the role and task of myth: to provide a sanitised account for the peace, but to cover up its true origin which would de-stabilise society. Because the true origin is never acknowledged, the peace that is achieved is a 'fake peace'.[17] Founded on a lie—the imputed guilt of the victim—the truce is unstable, liable to be rocked whenever desires and rivalries are re-awakened. At such times of societal crisis, order is again restored by repeating the myths that tell of the 'sacred' origins of society and by carrying out 'sacred' rituals that re-enact the original founding murder, or by finding new scapegoats to be similarly expelled/murdered.

Girard and his followers claim that the dynamics of mimesis and conflict resolved through violence to a victim underlie every civilisation and constitute every culture.[18] Bailie puts it as follows: 'Human culture as such begins with the community of victimisers looking at the corpse of its victim in solemn astonishment at the miracle of camaraderie that has just taken place'.[19] Religion, as a human cultural phenomenon, sacralises these dynamics. Hence the nexus of violence and religion—to which the popular myth testifies, as we have seen above.

Biblical narrative
However, Girard and his followers claim that in human history there is one exception that exposes the lie hidden under every cultural and religious account of the resolution of mimetic conflict though violence. Unlike human constructions of the idolatrous false sacred which are united *against* the victim, in the biblical narrative God is *for* the victim. 'The Bible is unique in its disclosure of the standpoint of the victim, which means that from the standpoint of the narrative, God takes the side of the victim.'[20] Alison argues that God is wholly other, not in rivalry with us, and therefore not subject to our conflictive games of for/against.[21]

---

17. Alison, Raising Abel, 21.
18. 'Human culture has its origin in a fratricidal murder, that of Abel by Cain, and all humans are by virtue of that origin radically distorted both in our willing and our knowing.' James Alison, *Faith Beyond Resentment: Fragments Catholic and Gay* (New York: Crossroad Publishing Company, 2001), 64.
19. Bailie, *Violence Unveiled*, 122
20. Williams, 'Foreword', xvii
21. Alison, *Undergoing God*, 4–5.

Where conflictive desires set up the dualities of good and bad, pure and impure, holy and profane, in-group and out-group, so that humans project all the negativity of the second of the above contrasting pairs onto the *guilty* victim who then merits (divine) punishment and justifies the community's expulsion/murder, the biblical narrative is alone in affirming that the victim is wholly *innocent*: 'the Jewish story . . . consists in the long, slow discovery of the innocence of the victim'.[22]

The implication of this discovery is that all the 'sacred' violence inflicted on the innocent down through the ages is a purely *human* projection. It has nothing to do with God. The lie about the imputed guilt of the victim is exposed once and for all.

Re-reading the biblical account through the Girardian lens of mimetic theory is nothing less than revolutionary. I will give two examples only.[23]

Abraham's 'sacrifice': The first is God's so-called 'test' of Abraham.[24] Traditional Jewish and Christian interpretations commend Abraham's willingness to sacrifice his first-born (legitimate) son as the epitome of faith,[25] as trusting in the creative power of God, and even as an anticipation of resurrection.[26] Islam and the *Qur'an* follow suit,[27] adding to the father's willingness the exemplary submission of the son.[28]

---

22. Alison, *Raising Abel*, 22.

23. For a detailed treatment see chapters 7–12 of Bailie, *Violence Unveiled*.

24. 'He said, "Take your son, your only son Isaac, whom you love, and go to the land of Moriah, and offer him there as a burnt offering on one of the mountains that I will show you"' (Gen 22:2). In the Islamic tradition the son is Ishmael.

25. 'Because you have done this, and have not withheld your son, your only son, I will indeed bless you (Gen 22:17) . . .' 'Was not our ancestor Abraham justified by works when he offered his son Isaac on the altar?' (Jam 2:21).

26. 'By faith Abraham, when put to the test, offered up Isaac. He who had received the promises was ready to offer up his only son, of whom he had been told, "It is through Isaac that descendants shall be named for you". He considered the fact that God is able even to raise someone from the dead—and figuratively speaking, he did receive him back (Heb 11:17–19).'

27. Islam traditionally situates the event on a mountain near Mecca, and ritually celebrates it in the annual Pilgrim Rituals culminating in ʿĪd al-Adhā (The Feast of Sacrifice).

28. Sūrah al-Saffāt 37:102ff has Abraham and his son both submit to God's command (and the verb is *aslamā*, the same word used for accepting Islam or becoming Muslims), in conformity with Islamic insistence on God's transcendence and on the

A Girardian reading of this pivotal event turns both the biblical text and its conventional interpretation upside down. Since violence is not from God, contrary to what the text states, it cannot be God who asks for human sacrifice.[29] Rather, according to the custom prevalent at that time, it was society who demanded human sacrifice to secure peace and prosperity.[30] However, Abraham refused to submit to society's expectation. Bailie states that his is a 'quintessentially biblical act'.[31]:

What we must try to see in the story of Abraham's non-sacrifice of Isaac is that Abraham's faith consisted, not of almost doing what he didn't do, but of *not* doing what he almost did, and not doing it in fidelity to the God in whose name his contemporaries thought it should be done.[32]

And again:

> The central issue of the story of Abraham's substitution of a ram for Isaac is precisely that, the issue of substitution. Abraham renounces human sacrifice and 'inaugurates' the ritual substitution of animals for humans.[33]

Abraham's faith did not consist in his *willingness to sacrifice* his son to establish peace and security, but in his *refusal to sacrifice* his son to satisfy society's expectations, a refusal based on faith that God is not a rival in conflict with Abraham's concern for his own offspring, but a provident God who cares for all. Confirmation of this interpretation is Abraham's prior assurance that 'God himself will provide the lamb for a burnt offering (Gen 22:8)', and his subsequent commemoration of the event by re-naming the place of (non-) sacrifice 'The Lord will provide (Gen 22:14)'.

---

power of his creative word: إِذَا قَضَى أَمْراً فَإِنَّمَا يَقُولُ لَهُ كُنْ فَيَكُونُ ، ' . . . when He has decreed a matter He only says to it "Be", and it is (Sūrah Mariam 19:35)'.

29. There are hints of this in the text. Gen 22:1 presents it as a 'test'. Gen 22:4 has the father giving assurance that he and the boy will both return from the mountain.

30. One could argue that human sacrifice is no less prevalent in our time—but now under the guise of unjust economic, social and political systems that lead to loss of human life and to environmental degradation that threatens the survival of the planet.

31. Bailie, *Violence Unveiled*, 141.

32. Bailie, *Violence Unveiled*, 141[italics in original].

33. Bailie, *Violence Unveiled*, 141.

Jesus' 'sacrifice': Although the original Anselmian theory of satisfaction is more subtle, popular imagination accounts for Jesus' sacrificial death more or less as follows: God created the universe and everything was good—but then came human sin. Since God is infinitely good, offence against God is also infinite, so although wanting to reconcile with fallen humanity, God's infinite mercy was constrained by God's infinite justice which demanded infinite satisfaction. God's dilemma was resolved when God's Word became incarnate—as human he truly represents the offending party, and as divine his reparation for sin is infinite, so he is able to satisfy God's justice. Jesus' death is the payment, the satisfaction, the atonement for our sin,[34] and since infinite justice is done, reconciliation is achieved, and the original relationship is restored.[35]

A Girardian reading turns the account of Jesus' sacrificial death around. The violence is not from God, and despite human pretensions to the contrary, never was. As always, the violence protects and reinforces human complicity in 'fratricidal fraternity'.[36] Jesus freely and deliberately takes the position of the victim precisely in order to expose the murderous lie, the mechanism of the violent sacred. Unlike Abraham, there is no intervening angel to stay the execution, which proceeds to its bloody climax, the death of the innocent son.[37] However, this is 'not a human sacrifice to God, but *God's sacrifice to humans*'.[38] It is God showing the infinite extent of divine love. God does not withhold even God's own son, who gives himself freely to satisfy, not God's, but *our blood lust*.

Jesus' resurrection is confirmation that the victim is wholly innocent; and that God has nothing to do with rivalry, anger, exclusion, vengeance, violence, and death (which are all principles of 'his world' under the dominion of death); that the living God is 'ineffable effervescence and vivacity, power, and deathlessness';[39] that God loves and accepts us as we are—*even as murderers*—precisely so that we no longer have to construct our security *over against* God or any other supposed rival, but may accept the freely-given love

---

34. Apart from the awkwardness of the sado-masochism involved, there are also questions about the morality of requiring someone to suffer for another, and about to whom the payment is made.

35. For a less dense summary see Alison, *Undergoing God*, 51–2.

36. Alison, 'Faith Beyond Resentment', 72.

37. The New Testament evidence is clear: 'I find no case against him (Jn 18:38, 19:4)'.

38. Alison, *Raising Abel*, 46 [italics mine].

39. Alison, *Raising Abel*, 40.

and life that God offers to all and be part of the Kingdom that is God's desire
from the beginning, as is written: 'For God so loved the world that he gave his
only Son, so that everyone who believes in him may not perish but may have
eternal life (Jn 3:6)'.

This alternative account of salvation is not just restoration of the old
creation, but a 'new creation' (2 Cor 5:17, Gal 6:15). Unlike the idolatrous
human construct based on sacred violence, this is the 'non-violent sacred',[40]
gracious gift of the living God, and antidote to all the violence in the world,
especially that associated with religion.

These few paragraphs suggest the significance of Girard's interpretation
for the perplexing nexus of violence and religion.[41] I now turn to my second
proposal.

Lonergan's stages of meaning
In his articles on meaning Lonergan normally distinguished *three* stages or
ideal types in the control of meaning. The stages are not strictly chronological,
for earlier forms can be found in later stages, but one cannot advance to the
later stages without going through the earlier stages.

> In the first stage conscious and intentional operations follow
> the mode of common sense. In the second stage besides the
> mode of common sense there is also the mode of theory,
> where theory is controlled by logic. In a third stage the
> modes of common sense and theory remain, science asserts
> its autonomy from philosophy, and there occur philosophies
> that leave theory to science and take their stand on
> interiority.[42]

Lonergan's account is characteristically dense. Late in his career he wrote a
more accessible account of shifts of meaning in relation to language, naming

---

40. Alison, *Raising Abel*, 107.
41. For detailed treatment of how the analysis is applied see the works of Alison and
    Bailie. For purposes of further research the bibliography also cites the English
    translations of Girard's original works.
42. Bernard JF Lonergan, SJ, *Method in Theology* (Toronto: University of Toronto
    Press, 1999), 85.

four developments: 'the linguistic, the literate, the logical, and the methodical'.[43]

Lonergan's four developments

1. The *linguistic* stage is the first step in the control of meaning. It fixes meaning with a spoken word—'this' (word) means 'that' (object). Meaning is thus fixed or stabilised. It is expressed through concrete *experience*, the shaped puff of air that signifies the intended object. This enables the control we exercise by naming the people and things in our world.[44]

2. The *literate* stage provides further control of meaning. By writing and reflecting on our formal propositions we gain greater competence and range in our use of words, putting them together to express more complex ideas that are not limited to our immediate senses. This greater control of meaning is achieved through greater *understanding*.

3. The *logical* stage applies to our written stories the clarity, coherence and rigor of logic. It leads to the organised systems of dictionary and grammar that iron out inconsistencies, stabilise the meanings even further and enable the systematic ordering and organising of meanings. Its final arbiter is *judgment*.

---

43. Bernard JF Lonergan, SJ, 'Philosophy and the Religious Phenomenon', in *Philosophical and Theological Papers 1965–1980*, edited by Robert C Croken and Robert M Doran (Toronto, Buffalo, London: University of Toronto Press, 2004), 404. For the provenance of these terms in Lonergan's earlier writings, especially the linguistic, see footnote 14, page 404. The first two are a distinction in his first stage of meaning mentioned above, while the last two correspond to his second and third stages of meaning. The four-fold schema can be correlated with the four ways in which consciousness works: experience, understanding, judging and choosing. This generative pattern of four types of operations is multiplied endlessly when applied to different fields. For example: the four stages of biological growth (infant, child, youth, adult).

44. For example: the significance of Adam's naming things in Genesis, and the significance of the Johannine 'in the beginning was the word'.

4. The *methodical* stage recognises the variety of systems of meanings
    and values that have emerged in our own lives, in history, and in
    different cultures, but even more it recognises that all these systems
    are the products of our own conscious operations, and most
    especially that in choosing them we have also been fashioning our
    own selves. It is accepting personal *responsibility* for our world and
    for who we have become, and for what we will make of our world
    and ourselves in the future. The methodical stage is our assuming
    personal responsibility for the ongoing process.

Significance of the stages

The significance for our topic of these stages is that world society is currently
in transition from the third logical stage of meaning to the fourth methodical
stage of meaning. Lonergan expresses it variously in different works as a shift
from the object to the subject,[45] from classicism to modernity, from culture
conceived normatively to culture conceived empirically, from the static to the
dynamic,[46] from nature to historicity.[47] The same idea of massive cultural
change is expressed by other authors in terms of 'paradigm shift'[48] and 'axial
age'.[49] I present three quotations from Lonergan to convey the basic idea:

> First, then, ours is a time of great social and cultural change.
> The relation of man to nature has been transformed by the

45. Bernard JF Lonergan, SJ, 'The Subject', in *A Second Collection: Papers by
    Bernard JF Lonergan, SJ,* edited by William FJ Ryan, SJ, and Bernard J Tyrrell, SJ
    (Toronto: University of Toronto Press, 1996), 69ff.
46. Bernard JF Lonergan, SJ, 'The Future of Christianity', in *A Second Collection*,
    159–63
47. Bernard JF Lonergan, SJ, 'Natural Right and Historical Mindedness', in *A Third
    Collection: Papers by Bernard JF Lonergan, SJ*, edited by Frederick E Crowe, SJ
    (Mahwah, New Jersey: Paulist Press, 1985), 170ff.
48. David J Bosch, *Transforming Mission: Paradigm Shifts in Theology of Mission*,
    volume 16, American Society of Missiology Series (New York: Orbis Books,
    1991).
49. 'The Axial Age was one of the most seminal periods of intellectual, psychological,
    philosophical, and religious change in recorded history; there would be nothing
    comparable until the Great Western Transformation, which created our own
    scientific and technological modernity.' Karen Armstrong, *The Great Trans-
    formation: The Beginning of Our Religious Traditions* (New York, Toronto: Alfred
    A Knopf, 2006), xii.

discoveries of natural science, the flood of inventions, the know-how of technicians, the enterprise of industrialists, businessmen, financiers. Earlier ways of living have been disrupted by urbanism, increasing longevity, a population explosion, built-in obsolescence, mobility, detached and functional relations between persons, universal, prolonged and continuing education, instantaneous information, increasing leisure and travel, perpetually available entertainment. There is a distinctive meaning conveyed by the phrase 'modern living'. It connotes a varying set of more or less established innovations in the family and in manners, in society and in education, in the state and in the law, in the economy and in technology, in the Churches and the sects.[50]

Concomitant with this transformation [to the modern notion of science] has been the even more radical transformation in human studies. Man is to be known not only in his nature but also in his historicity, not only philosophically but also historically, not only abstractly but also concretely.[51]

In the introduction to his account of *The Origins of Modern Science* Herbert Butterfield noted that the scientific revolution in the sixteenth and seventeenth centuries overturned the authority in science not only of the middle ages but also of the ancient world. He concluded that the revolution 'outshines everything since the rise of Christianity and reduces the Renaissance and Reformation to the rank of mere episodes, mere internal displacements within the system of medieval Christendom'. [52]

Conclusion

I conclude by bringing the insights of the two authors together. From Lonergan, society is *in a time of crisis* of cultural transition from one stage of meaning to another; from Girard, *in a time of crisis* people feel insecure and

---

50. Bernard JF Lonergan, SJ, 'Belief: Today's Issue', in *A Second Collection*, 90.
51. Lonergan, 'Natural Right and Historical Mindedness', 179.
52. Bernard JF Lonergan, SJ, 'The Ongoing Genesis of Methods', in *A Third Collection*, 147. Lonergan's endnote: 'Herbert Butterfield, *The Origins of Modern Science,* 1965, p. vii'.

threatened and resolve their dilemma by uniting and lashing out against victims.

I propose that this is exactly what is happening in our day. Remember that the first recorded murder in mythical history is also situated in a time of transition, from pastoral living to agricultural living, for Abel offered animal sacrifice, while Cain offered the fruits of harvest.[53] It is not surprising that there would be much bloodshed in a time of such vast, rapid and far-reaching change as we are currently undergoing.

The antipathy is not so much between different religions, the Samuel Huntington 'clash of civilisations' theory. Rather it is between radically different approaches to meaning across all the religions. The so-called 'fundamentalists' or 'extremists' are holding on to precious values, and are resistant to change, but insofar as their fixed ideas take priority, then people become expendable. The so-called 'liberals' or 'moderns' are looking for new expression, and open to change, but insofar as novelty takes priority then the tradition and its defenders become dismissible. What is needed is for the antagonistic rivals to set aside their mutual animosity and discover the genuine meaning and value that each is trying to promote.

Since what I am grasping at is the dawn of a new era, and it is yet early, and still dark (see Jn 20:1), it is not possible to see clearly the transformed society that a new pacific way of relating between believers from different religions will forge. So to point in that direction I revert to an ancient parable:

> The story is told of a Jewish rabbi whose disciples were debating the question of when precisely 'daylight' commenced. The one ventured the proposal: 'It is when one can see the difference between a sheep and a goat at a distance'. Another suggested, 'It is when you can see the difference between a fig tree and an olive tree at a distance'. And so it went on. When they eventually asked the Rabbi for his view, he said, 'When one human being looks into the face of another and says, "This is my sister, or this is my brother", then the night is over and the day has begun'.[54]

---

53. Bailie, *Violence Unveiled*, 138–40. I am confident that research will confirm that all the major religions of the world emerged when society was in the crisis of transition (for example: rupture from the previous tradition), and that the major reforms they underwent all occurred in transitional crises.
54. Cited at <http://www.crosscurrents.org/Esack.htm>.

A Short Bibliography

Alison, James, *Faith Beyond Resentment: Fragments Catholic and Gay* (New York: Crossroad, 2001).

————, *The Joy of Being Wrong: Original Sin through Easter Eyes* (New York: Crossroad, 1998).

————, *On Being Liked* (London: Darton, Longman & Todd, 2003).

————, *Raising Abel: The Recovery of Eschatological Imagination* (New York: Crossroad, 1996.

————, *Undergoing God: Dispatches from the Scene of a Break-In* (New York, London: Continuum, 2006).

Armstrong, Karen, *The Great Transformation: The Beginning of Our Religious Traditions*, (New York, Toronto: Alfred A Knopf, 2006).

Bailie, Gil, *Violence Unveiled: Humanity at the Crossroads* (New York: Crossroad, 1995).

Bosch, David J, *Transforming Mission: Paradigm Shifts in Theology of Mission,* 16, American Society of Missiology Series (New York: Orbis Books, 1991).

Girard, René, *I See Satan Fall Like Lightning*, translated by Williams JG (New York: Orbis Books, 2001).

————, *The Scapegoat* (Baltimore: Johns Hopkins University Press, 1986).

————, *A Theatre of Envy*, second edition (Leominster, Herefordshire: Gracewing, 2000).

————, *Things Hidden Since the Foundation of the World*, translated by Stephen Bann and Michael Metteer (Stanford, California: Stanford University Press, 1987).

————, *Violence and the Sacred*, translated by Patrick Gregory (Baltimore: Johns Hopkins University Press, 1977).

Kirwan, Michael, *Discovering Girard* (London: Darton, Longman & Todd, 2004).

Lonergan, Bernard JF, SJ, 'Belief: Today's Issue', in *A Second Collection*: *Papers by Bernard JF Lonergan, SJ,* edited by William FJ Ryan, SJ and Bernard J Tyrrell, SJ (Toronto: University of Toronto Press, 1996), 87–99.

————, 'The Future of Christianity', in *A Second Collection: Papers by Bernard JF Lonergan, SJ*, edited by William FJ Ryan, SJ and Bernard J Tyrrell, SJ (Toronto: University of Toronto Press, 1996), 149–63.

————, *Method in Theology* (Toronto: University of Toronto Press, 1999).

————, 'Natural Right and Historical Mindedness', in *A Third Collection: Papers by Bernard JF Lonergan, SJ* edited by Frederick E Crowe, SJ (Mahwah New Jersey: Paulist Press, 1985), 169–83.

————, 'The Ongoing Genesis of Methods', in *A Third Collection: Papers by Bernard JF Lonergan SJ*, edited by Frederick E Crowe, SJ (New York: Paulist Press, 1985), 146–65.

————, 'Philosophy and the Religious Phenomenon', in *Philosophical and Theological Papers 1965–1980*, edited by Robert C Croken and Robert M Doran (Toronto, Buffalo, London: University of Toronto Press, 2004), 391–408.

————, 'The Subject', in *A Second Collection: Papers by Bernard JF Lonergan SJ*, edited by William FJ Ryan, SJ and Bernard J Tyrrell, SJ (Toronto: University of Toronto Press, 1996), 69–86.

Williams, James G, 'Foreword', in *I See Satan Fall Like Lightning* (New York: Crossroad, 2001).

2

Building Communities of Peace in the Midst of Violence: An Intercultural Approach in Christian Theology

James Haire

The contemporary reality of many parts of the world is one of deep violence. The irony of the ending of the Cold War is that it has coincided with the unleashing of uncontrollable violence in many parts of the world. The combination of high technology and seemingly medieval tribal conflict has become the pattern of our times. Behind all of this lies the development of a new ideology, particularly in the West, which 'legitimatizes a culture of violence by invoking God arbitrarily to suit a particular agenda for aggression. As a result, insecurity, fear and anxiety characterize the lives of many people'[1] throughout the world.

This culture of violence manifests itself in many different ways.

There is the negative impact of economic globalisation, which continues to widen the gap between the haves and the have-nots. There is also the structural violence of domineering or negligent governments in relation to their populations. Corruption and the abuse of power often manifest themselves in violence. In addition, there are often structural forms of traditional violence, mainly based in patriarchal societies. These result in gender discrimination, forced labour migration, discrimination against young people and those with disabilities, and discrimination based on race, caste, and class. Surrounding our very life is the violence against the environment.

Against this rather gloomy picture, positive signs must also be noted. There is a yearning among young people for true manifestations of peace and of peaceful communities. In the aftermath of the devastating tsunami in 2004 we have observed remarkable efforts to create communities of peace in

---

1. S Kobia, quoted in World Council of Churches News Release entitled 'Restating the Ecumenical Vision demands Conversion, says Kobia', Geneva, 15 February 2005. See J Burton, *Conflict: Resolution and Prevention* (London: Macmillan Press, 1990), 1–2, 13–24.

various places. Again, the speed of reconciliation after ethnic and communal violence often has been very rapid. Despite violence, there is evidence of a vast amount of resilience among populations who have been deeply wounded.

In 2001 and 2002, I revisited Halmahera in the North Moluccas in Indonesia, where I had served for thirteen years in the 1970s and 1980s, and saw the results of the Christian-Muslim violence, which had been stimulated by the political situation in Indonesia at that time, and aggravated by elements within the Indonesian military. Events too terrible for words had occurred. Both Muslims and Christians were involved in the violence. Let me just give one example. Six of my former students in Indonesia, all ordained pastors, were killed. One of them was the Rev Albert Lahi. He was in the vestry of his parish church when elements of the *Jihad*, aided and abetted by elements of the military, arrived. He knew that his case was hopeless. He asked to be allowed to pray. His wish was granted. He put on his preaching gown and knelt by the communion table. He prayed for his church, for his nation, for his congregation and for those about to kill him. The Sunday School children who observed the whole incident told me what happened. Then he stretched his head forward and was beheaded. His head was carried on a pole around the village. His body was dragged by the feet for all to see. Yet in this same village, and in this whole area, reconciliation has come about. Christians too, were heavily engaged in violence. However, since 2002 both the Muslim and the Christian populations have been slowly but surely working their futures out together, in a quite remarkable display of creating communities of peace.

The Uniting Church in Australia, in co-operation with Churches in Asia and the Pacific, has developed a program entitled *Young Ambassadors for Peace (YAP)*. Here, young people from conflict situations—in the Moluccas (Indonesia), Bougainville (Papua New Guinea), the Highlands of Papua New Guinea, the Solomon Islands, North-East India, and Sri Lanka—have developed communities of reconciliation in each of their regions. These communities have developed across ethnic, religious, caste, and class divisions.

Against the situation in which we find ourselves—in which we find incredible violence within our communities, but also the resilience of the human spirit—we need to find an intercultural approach in Christian theology towards *building communities of peace in the midst of violence*.

That we should investigate this is important, for two reasons. Firstly, as Christianity represents just over one third of the global population, it has a responsibility for the existence of violence in our contemporary world. Secondly, despite its strong peace traditions, Christianity has been involved in violence in much of its history. Within this, we need to hear the voice of God because that is central to our identity as Christians.

How do we listen to the voice of God? It is not our task primarily to invoke God for our particular view of the world, but rather, in humility, to sit and listen as that divine voice comes to us.

Therefore, in looking at how we may build communities of peace, let us, in this paper, take up this task theologically, as we must as Christians. Let us first go to the very heart of our existence as Christians, and as the church. The inexplicable will of God to be for, and with, humanity implies that the church's life cannot begin to be understood in terms of the structures and events of the world. Equally, God's inexplicable will to be God with and for humanity implies that we should always understand our life as Christians theologically. These simple, yet profound, facts derive from the mystery of the triune God not to be God apart from, or separate from, humanity, but rather to make God's very being intersect with the unity of the Son of God with us. Our theological basis, as Christians and as the church, is in the wonder of God's condescension, in the intentionality of God's solidarity with sinners— that is, with those who find their self-identity solely within themselves, and find their self-justification and solace in themselves alone, without any reference to God. The church is called to exist solely through the solidarity of Jesus Christ with those who are alienated from God, by Christ going to the extremes of alienation for humanity, so that humanity might, through Christ, come close to God. At the heart of our faith is expressed the fact that God does not wish to be alone in celebrating the wonder of God's inexpressible love for humanity. God in Christ calls into existence an earthly Body of the Son who is its heavenly Head, in order that humanity may responsively rejoice with God in the harmony and peace which God has established for creation.

If the being of the church and its life is predicated upon the grace of Jesus Christ as itself defining God's action in the world for the reconciliation of creation, including humanity, then its life of peace is that which it receives from Christ, who is its life. The church's very existence will be shaped by the manner in which it confesses this truth to be its very life.

On the basis of our theological identity in Christ, we take the New Testament writings, on Christian community especially, most seriously. Like our struggle to be faithful disciples of Christ to-day in a world of violence, Christianity was born in a milieu of political and social violence. The evidence which we have both from the New Testament and from non-Christian sources of the first century CE points to the constant struggle of Christianity to survive in such a climate. Clearly that climate of violence also influenced the language and concept-construction of many parts of the New Testament. Nevertheless, it is also very striking how early Christianity sought to transcend this violent world.

A microcosm of the New Testament understanding of building communities of peace for all can be seen in the ethical sections of Paul's writings, especially in those ethical sections in his *Letter to the Romans*.

It is arguable that no document in Christian history has played a more influential part than Paul's *Letter to the Romans*. One simply has to reflect on the pivotal impact of *Romans*: on Augustine and the development of Western Christianity; on Luther and then on Calvin and Cranmer and the political, social, and religious consequences of the Reformation; on Wesley and the emergence of the evangelical revival; on Karl Barth and his dominance of twentieth century theology; and on the Second Vatican Council and the renewal of the Roman Catholic Church. A primary impetus for Augustine, Luther, Calvin, Cranmer, Wesley, Barth, and the members of Vatican II came from Paul's writings, particularly from *Romans*. This letter is thus central to Christian self-identity and self-understanding. It forms a useful basis for the exploration of the understanding of Christian community based on identification with God in Christ as it challenges the prevailing Greco-Roman culture of status based on potentially violent concepts through the ethical sections of *Romans*, particularly Chapter 12.

In order to understand this ideal community culture, we need to understand that it both reacts against, and transforms, Greco-Roman cultures of the first century CE. We need, first, of course, to look at the results of recent research on the social organisation, social interaction, and religious organisations of this time.

Firstly, in the world of early Christianity, social groupings were based on kinship, ethnic issues, power, and politics. Kinship was the central factor of social organisation. The kinship group was the focus of individual loyalty, and had decisive influence over individual identity and self-awareness. The security of each individual was grounded in the community, sharing as they did common interests, values, and activities. Hence, the most basic unit of social awareness was not the individual. Individual consciousness was subordinate to social consciousness.[2]

---

2.   BJ Malina, *The New Testament World: Insights from Cultural Anthropology* (Atlanta: John Knox Press, 1981), 55–66, 60–4; WA Meeks, *The First Urban Christians: The Social World of the Apostle Paul* (New Haven: Yale University Press, 1983), 90–1. See also G Theissen, *Social Reality and the Early Christians:*

Secondly, religion, like other social factors, was enmeshed in kinship and politics. Membership of a religious community was not necessarily based on religious relationships, but on bonds of kinship that gave structure to religious associations. Membership in religious groups was either involuntary or voluntary. Involuntary members belonged to a religion because, for example, they were born into a particular family. Voluntary membership in early Christianity stood in contrast to family-based religion. In the first century CE, the religion of voluntary members resulted in a newly-created kinship group.[3] Although it appeared to be similar to, or to look like, any other kinship group, it was in fact a created or fictive kinship grouping. In early Christianity, language of the natural kinship group, for example 'household (of faith)', was used for a created kinship group. Indeed, the struggle of the Christian community as a totality, for example in Rome, can be seen in relationship to these two types. It struggled as to which of these two types it in fact belonged.

Thirdly, there is considerable evidence in the first century CE, within Greco-Roman culture, of intense expressions of emotion, through outbursts of anger, aggression, pugnacity, and indeed violence. Moreover, these appear to have been socially acceptable.[4]

Fourthly, in such an atmosphere, concern for honour and shame was significant. This was because honour determined social standing and was essential for social cooperation. Honour was the outward approval given to a group or an individual by others whose honour was not in question. The honour of an individual normally was dependent upon the outward approval given to one's group. On the other hand, people became shamed when they transgressed group standards or when they sought a social status to which public approval was not given. Honour was ascribed, for example, by birth into an honourable family, or by it being given or bestowed from honourable persons of power. It was acquired by outdoing others in social interchange. A

Theology, Ethics and the World of the New Testament (Edinburgh: T&T Clark, 1992), 272–8.

3. G Theissen, *The Social Setting of Pauline Christianity: Essays on Corinth*, edited and translated by John H Schutz (Philadelphia: Fortress, 1982), 27–40. See also PF Esler, *The First Christians in their Social Worlds: Social-Scientific Approaches to New Testament Interpretation* (London and New York: Routledge, 1994), 6–12.

4. L Pearson, *Popular Ethics in Ancient Greece* (Stanford: University Press, 1973), 193; AJM Wedderburn, *The Reason for Romans: Studies of the New Testament and its World* (Edinburgh: T&T Clark, 1988) 81–3. See also WRG Loader, *Jesus' Attitude towards the Law: A Study of the* Gospels (Grand Rapids, Michigan and Cambridge, United Kingdom: Eerdmans, 2002), 177.

person's sense of self-worth was therefore established by public reputation related to that person's associations rather than by a judgment of conscience.[5]

Over against these four factors of community life in the Greco-Roman cultures of the first century CE, Paul summons Christians to a new form of religious organization—a fictive kinship religious community based on identity in Christ in which membership is voluntary—and also to new social roles. These social roles are based on the twin concepts of peace or harmony, and mercy, in a complex of cultures where expressions of violence seem not only to have been common, but also accepted, as has been noted.

To understand the significance of peace or harmony, and the related concept of mercy, in Paul's writings, it is helpful firstly to look more widely in the New Testament at the Greek words commonly translated as *peace* and *mercy*.

There are strong communal elements in the New Testament uses of *peace* and of *mercy*. There are also strong elements of God's desire for a world which ultimately is to be under God's rule. These factors we see as we look at the two concepts more closely.

The Greek word *eirēnē* means *harmony* and *peace*. The verb *eirēneuō* signifies *to be at peace* or *to live at peace* or *to keep the peace*. *Eirēnē* is also closely associated with the Hebrew term for *peace* and *harmony*, *shalôm*. In the New Testament, *eirēnē* refers to two distinct states of peace.

Firstly, it means the final salvation and harmony of the whole community, and thus of the whole of each individual person. Zechariah proclaims this expected state of salvation and harmony of the whole community in Luke 1: 76–9. The Angels' Song in Luke 2: 14 refers to this salvation and harmony which has come to the earth. This concept is again referred to in Hebrews 13: 20–1. It is this idea of peace which Paul himself uses in II Corinthians 5: 16–19. There he speaks about Christian believers, being justified by grace in faith, having peace with God through Christ. These believers, Paul says, will be granted salvation. So the concept has a future orientation, referring to the final end of history.

Secondly, on the basis of its future orientation, *eirēnē* refers to a condition here and now of peace and harmony, guaranteed by what will occur at the end of time. This divinely-willed state in the here and now includes Christians' well-being, and their harmony with God, with one another and with all human beings. This idea appears in Hebrews 12: 14. Paul uses it in Ephesians 4: 1–3. So, again, the concept has also a present orientation. This present orientation

---

5. Malina, *The New Testament World*, 27–48.

refers in the first instance to the state of the whole Christian community, and then to the individual as part of it.

The first-century CE Greek terms for *mercy* are *oiktirmos* and *eleos*. Both refer to *mercy* and *compassion*, while *oiktirmos* additionally means *pity*. The verbs *eleeō* and *eleaō* mean *to show kindness* or *to be merciful*. Human mercy, therefore, denotes the divinely intended attitude of Christians towards each other. It signifies sympathy and loving-kindness, which are to be exhibited in relationships, particularly through acts of help to the needy. This we see in Matthew 9: 13, in relation to Jesus' attitude to eating with outsiders, and in Luke 10: 37, in relation to Jesus defining the neighbour who may be an outsider. The neighbour was the despised outsider who showed mercy to the person on the road from Jerusalem to Jericho who fell among thieves.

Thus, in the definitions of both of these terms as they were used in the New Testament we see sustained communal elements, and also sustained pointers to the ideal of a society which is ultimately to be under God's rule. An example of this is in Romans 12: 1 where Paul describes Christian life against the background of these terms, using metaphors from the sacrificial cult. This cult spoke of the offering of the central parts of a community's life to the power of God. For Christians, this is now to suggest that Christians are to give themselves permanently to the rule of God, as this way has been opened for them through God's self-sacrifice in Christ. The sacrificial cult continues to point to the rule of God throughout the community. It also points to an individual's relationship with God within the community's relationship with God. This is based on Paul's theological argument in Romans 5: 1 and 9–10, where he describes how *peace* (*eirēnē*) and *reconciliation* (*katallagē*) have been given by God to God's community in Christ.

So, if we now return to Paul, and specifically to *Romans*, we can observe how he deals with the four factors of community life in Greco-Roman culture as outlined above.

Over against these four factors outlined above, Paul summons Christians to new social roles. They are based on mercy, peaceable conduct and reconciliation in a culture where expressions of violence seem to have been normative. The call for transformation now means new expressions of group identity. No longer based on kinship or ethnicity, group identity nevertheless seeks to retain the intense cohesion of former groups. Paul's community members bind themselves together as one body in Christ. This metaphor is poignantly suitable in a society where self-awareness arises from group association rather than from individual worth. The ideals of honourable and shameless conduct are altered in that they are not primarily derived from society outside. Rather, enhanced honour for the community derives from its incorporation into its risen Lord. Patterns of social co-operation are modified as a result. A new communal identity as one body in Christ is thus reinforced.

The social groupings see their identity as coming from beyond themselves. Their self-understanding and their life together are defined by the kindness or mercy of God and by the truthful harmony (or peace) which God gives. The other factors in the transformation include cohesiveness within the group based on an understanding of God's action from outside. For that reason, attitudes of peaceful harmony are central to the community's identity. Moreover, no other identity marker (ethnicity, gender, class, or status) may be accepted as absolute. Honour derives from the faith-life of the community, originating from beyond. The original groupings are transformed by the new ideal of a central awareness of their relationship with God.

In addition, throughout the ethical sections of *Romans* attitudes to those *outside* the newly created Christian social groupings are to be the same as to those *within* them. There is to be no distinction. All are to be treated in the same way.

We thus see the radical way in which Paul took hold of Greco-Roman categories of group identity, and then applied to them new metaphors, including that of the body of Christ, so as to create in them a totally new identity. Present-day individualism makes it difficult for us to see the significance of the dynamism of Paul's transformation of a received aggressive culture. Moreover, throughout world history, Christianity has had both success and failure in being able to present and live out this newly transformed identity in Christ. To this varying success and failure, and the reasons behind it, we now turn.

Let us look through one particular lens at the processes of the spread and development of world Christianity. Let us see how the category of peace, and the ideal of communities of peace, developed on the one hand, or were restricted on the other, as Christianity expanded. Christianity was born within an immediate Jewish cultural environment, surrounded by an Aramaic and Hebrew vocabulary, and Semitic expectations. However, this integrated Judaism, in its strict and official vesture, rejected Jesus of Nazareth and later turned against Paul as he championed freedom from the Law through Jesus Christ. As the New Testament and second and third century CE writings demonstrate, Christianity penetrated much more easily into Hellenistic culture, including Hellenistic Judaism, than into the culture of Judaism itself. From Hellenism Christianity developed into the wider Greco-Roman culture, and subsequently moved into Northern and Eastern Europe, in addition to its movements into Asia. Why was it that it found its movement into Hellenism much easier than its movement into Judaism? It was because Hellenism was more of a culture in the original sense of that word than Judaism. Hellenism was much more related to primarily agricultural societies whose deepest concern was with being in harmony with nature. The Christ Event spoke of birth, growth, development, maturity, death, resurrection, and new life. This was a cycle. It fitted the cyclic world of agricultural life. It was a cyclic culture. That world spoke of planting, development, maturity, harvest (or death), new life, renewed fertility of the soil, and new growth. The Jesus story fitted the pattern of agricultural life. It had also been similar to the Old Testament dramas of the Prophets and Psalms, where they had spoken of destruction and rebirth.

However, in the Judaism of the first and second century CE, a different world had emerged. There was no longer the drama of the Old Testament Prophets and Psalms. First and second century CE Judaism tended to stress the precise following of particular divinely-inspired words, which had been uttered up until the time of Ezra and the 'Men of the Great Synagogue' and thereafter had ceased.[6]

So the gospel lived and flourished in a cyclic and agricultural mode, as it was interwoven into agricultural societies. In this way, on the whole, the gospel moved north and west, in addition to its movement east. However, it did not enter the world of Judaism to any large degree. As it moved west and north and east, the transformation of agricultural society meant that the gospel was totally interwoven into the fabric of the culture. It also began to mould and to direct the cyclic impulses of the culture. Wholeness, harmony, rhythm, and ritual (to do with water, and around a thanksgiving meal, for example) were the means by which the gospel was expressed. Baptism was the water ritual; Holy Communion was the thanksgiving ritual. Both were central means of expressing the faith. Many parts of central, northern and western Europe were evangelised in this way. The movement was slow and halting. Yet the interweaving continued. Celtic Christianity developed in this way—deeply cyclic, and deeply agricultural. There were movements also into western Asia, to India and to areas further east where Christianity developed in this way in the first millennium.

---

6. As in the first words of the *Pirqê Abôth* ('The Fathers'). See H Danby, *The Mishnah*, translated from the Hebrew by H Danby, (Oxford: Clarendon Press, 1933), 446–61.

There was, of course, from time to time, resistance to the gospel, but on the whole the development of Christianity was communal. Christianity thrived in this cyclic world, and expressed itself communally. There were internal communities of peace, and frequently relations of peace with surrounding faiths. However, another world existed in which Christianity had not been able to develop so well. This was the world of a trading- and word-culture, the world developed by first and second century CE Judaism into which Christianity was not able to develop throughout the first millennium. However, with the rise of travel and trade, Christianity itself began to develop into a trading- and word-culture, a culture in which wholeness, community, harmony and ritual received less attention, and more attention was given to common standards to guide diverse peoples as they sought to live together. The development of trading- and word-cultures occurred largely in the period from the fourteenth century CE, often referred to as the 'Modern Period', taking in as it did the European expansion in trade and commerce, the Renaissance and the Reformation, and industrial modernisation.

This was a world quite different from that of the agricultural world. Journeying individuals and communities needed clear-cut ordinances in warding off their dangers and temptations, far from the cyclic life of the soil which they had left behind. That cyclic world had been so clearly transfigured by the Christ Event, and celebrated in ritual as a means of expression and teaching. The trade- and word-culture was different. Guidelines were needed to bind communities together. Doctrine, ethics, church polity, and management were all important. The emphasis was to be on the Book (the Bible), the Guide to the Book (Confessions and Catechisms), and the Interpreter of the Book (the Preacher).

Parallel cultural emphases occurred in other trade and word religions, specifically Judaism and Islam. In Christianity, in this word and trade form, there is emphasis on the Bible, the Confession and Catechism, and the Preacher. In Judaism, there is a parallel emphasis on the Torah, the Mishnah and Talmud, and the Rabbi. In Islam, there is a parallel emphasis on the *Qur'an*, the *Sharī'ah*, and the *Faqīh*.

So now Christianity succeeded in operating in two cultural modes: the cyclic- and agricultural-mode on the one hand, and the word- and trade-mode on the other. However, the critical issue arose during the period of evangelisation, from the late eighteenth century CE onwards. Could Christianity, which largely existed in a word and trade cultural mode in the mission-active nations, translate itself again into the cyclic and agricultural cultural modes of the receptor cultures? If the mission-active cultures had been those that were still in the original cyclic and agricultural mode moving into new cyclic and agricultural receptor cultures, then the spread of the gospel would have been relatively simple. However, mainly they were not. They were trade- and word-cultures. In the process of evangelisation a variety of reactions occurred. In some situations, the spread of the gospel was highly successful, as, for example, in many parts of the Outer Islands of Indonesia, in north-east India, in much of the Pacific, and in parts of the African continent. In other situations, it was extremely difficult, as, for example, in Japan, in parts of India, and in parts of China.

In the development of Christianity in the cyclic and agricultural mode, great emphasis was placed on the baptising of communities and cultures into the faith. Once whole Christian communities had been established, then there tended to be harmony and peace both within those communities and in relation to the surrounding societies. However, although trade- and word-culture communities encouraged peace *within* their community, they did not necessarily encourage community with those *outside* the faith-group. Often colonial Protestant communities were internally cohesive, but aggressive towards the world around them, including toward indigenous religions. So in the West Indies and in the Southern states of the United States, the local population was enslaved, or slaves imported, and the slaves simply acquiesced in the colonists' religion. There was little attempt to translate the gospel into the indigenous community. In Australia, minimal attempt was made to translate the gospel into Indigenous cultural terms. In China, Japan, and India, parts of the population were antagonised by Christianity.[7]

This stands in stark contrast to the teachings of the New Testament, epitomised in Paul as we have seen, where Paul's ethics for *internal* Christian life are exactly the same as his ethics for those *outside*. You treat the outsider in exactly the same way as you treat your Christian sister or brother.

Now we come again to the issue of communities of peace. In ecumenical and evangelical terms, we need the gospel in both cyclic and word cultures. Where the church has been primarily related to an agricultural- or cyclic-culture, it needs the struggle with the divine graceful criticism of that

---

7. See, for example, RHS Boyd, *India and the Latin Captivity of the Church: The Cultural Context of the Gospel*, monograph supplement to the *Scottish Journal of Theology*, number 3 (London: Cambridge University Press, 1974), 117–19; J Haire, *The Character and Theological Struggle of the Church in Halmahera, Indonesia, 1941–1979*, *Studien zur interkulturellen Geschichte des Christentums*, Band 26 (Frankfurt am Main und Bern: Lang, 1981), 322–3.

transfiguration in order to be *semper reformanda*. It needs to hear the voice in word form to be constantly reformed. Equally, a church which is primarily related to the gospel in a word- or trade-culture, needs always the struggle with the divine fact of incarnation, that God has placed God's church in the world.

However, we need to be aware that the existence of the church in word- and trade-cultures has a tendency to work against building communities of peace.

This is frequently so across religious divides. Thus it is especially so where there is a meeting between two word- or trading-culture religions. There are four poignant examples of this. First, it is seen in the struggle between the strident word-culture form of Judaism and the word-culture form of Islam in the Middle East. Second, is observed in the violence of the past between Muslims and Christians in urban areas of Indonesia. Third, it is seen in the attack of word-culture Christianity against the word- and trading-culture of Judaism in Nazi Germany. Fourth, it is observed in the antagonism between specific traditions of Islam and certain traditions of Christianity in the United States.

Therefore, a number of things are incumbent upon us.

Firstly, we need to be aware that creating communities of peace from the Pauline tradition means creating attitudes of peace and harmony towards those *outside* who are the same as to those *within* the faith-community.

Secondly, we need to be aware that Christianity needs both its cyclic- or agricultural-culture forms on the one hand, and its word- and trade-culture forms on the other. However, we need to be aware that its word- and trade-culture forms have a tendency to go against the New Testament, and specifically Pauline, teaching, in that they can tend to have an aggressive attitude towards those *outside the community*, while fostering cohesiveness within the faith-group.

Thirdly, we need to stress the importance of cyclic- and agricultural-culture forms within the varied expressions of Christianity, and to see how word- and trade-culture expressions of Christianity can in our time be translated into cyclic forms.

Fourthly, contextual theology, therefore, is not simply a matter of engaging in word-culture exercises (in, for example, doctrine, ethics and polity). It is as much an expression of faith through liturgy, drama, dance, music, and communal living.

Fifthly, the communal nature of expressing theology in many parts of the world calls Christians in particular to advance, at all opportunities, the eight goals of the Millennial Declaration (MDG) of the United Nations, that is, to:

1. eradicate poverty and hunger;
2. achieve universal primary education;
3. promote gender equality and empower women;
4. reduce child mortality;
5. improve maternal health;
6. combat HIV/AIDS, malaria and other diseases;
7. ensure environmental sustainability; and
8. develop a global partnership for development.[8]

These are indeed expressions of genuine *theologiae in locō.*

Sixthly, this way of communal harmony is necessary in the ways in which the churches throughout the world live their lives. Consensus decision-making, mutual celebration, the interest in others' rituals and festivities are important in the varied international ways of being Christian.

Seventhly, truth can be communicated without aggression. Therefore, the ecumenical movement throughout the world, in and of itself, as it brings the churches together, is central to the creation of peaceful communities.

We in our time live in a deeply ambivalent age, an age of high technology and of medieval conflict, and an age as strangely confident of the saving powers of the market-place as a previous age was strangely confident of the saving powers of collectivism. Yet both these ages have reflected inbuilt cultures of violence. In this age, Christians are called to follow Paul in speaking of, and living out, the wonder of God's mercy, peaceful harmony and reconciliation with humanity. Christians are thus called to a life of praise, which embraces all of our personal and social life, in all its practical, ethical, religious, political and intellectual aspects. That praise will be both culture-transforming and culture-renewing, over against the self-worship of individuals and nations in our time. As we seek models to overcome violence around the globe, Paul's picture of the Christian community as a vehicle of transformation to overcome violence is a powerful and liberating word.

This Pauline vision of Christian community is eschatological in nature. It pictures the end of time as now already beginning to be operative. One of the great leaders of the ecumenical movement, Archbishop William Temple,

---

8. See <http://www.un.org/millennium goals/>.

served as Archbishop of Canterbury for only two years from 1942 to 1944. When he arrived in Canterbury, he was already ill. One of his lasting images to the ecumenical movement was that of the Christian with bi-focal lenses. In his writing he says that we should look through the top part of our glasses to see the church as God intends it to be, fully united. With the bottom of our lenses we see the church as it actually is, divided. Although we look at the church day by day with the bottom part of our spectacles, we should also always live as if the top part were reality, as if the church was already completely united.

So it is with communities of peace. With the top part of our spectacles, as it were, we see a world community of peace and harmony. With the lower part of our spectacles, we observe the world as it is. Although we daily look at reality through the lower part, we must live as if the upper part is reality too. In the church, we have to model what fully harmonious and peaceful communities are. For that reason we need to use consensus models of discussion. We need in our churches to model peaceful debate, and to celebrate peace. For Christians, it is not just *what* we do, but *how* we do *what* we do that is important. Just for a moment, think of the violence of language structures and procedures in your church. How can we speak of peace throughout the world unless we model it? Perhaps the greatest enculturation or *theologia in locō* which we need is to express the style of our theological existence through forms of communities of peace. Our Western inheritances have not always helped us in this. Nor indeed have some of the inheritances of many cultures. The way we express theology, the way in which we preach, the ways in which we engage in the worship of God, the ways in which we engage in community services, the ways we live need to express this *shalôm*.

One Saturday afternoon in the city of Belfast, a bank was robbed by a terrorist group. During a car chase, the car in which the terrorists were involved and the police car following were both engaged in an accident. A mother was pushing a pram along the road, holding her toddler in her hand, with her baby in the pram. One of the cars slammed into them, and the two children were killed instantly. The mother's name was Betty Williams, and she had a friend, a social worker named Miréad Corrigan. The two of them, as a result of this appalling accident, formed a group called the Peace People. Subsequently both of them went on to receive the Nobel Peace Prize.

I was involved on my leave from Indonesia with this group, trying to build a community of peace in Ireland. Although within Christianity, it tragically represented all the elements of inter-faith and ethnic violence. To overcome this, we sought to live out a single community of peace. When a Protestant was killed, Catholic clergymen would carry the person's coffin into the Protestant church for the funeral service. When a Catholic was killed, Protestant clergy would carry that person's coffin into the Catholic church for the funeral service. One Saturday afternoon we were engaged in the regular marches which became a pattern of those times, walking through Protestant and Catholic areas, so as to show our unity in Christ. I had a friend who had been teaching scholastic philosophy at the University in Belfast and had recently become a bishop. His name was Cahal Daly. He subsequently became Cardinal Archbishop of Armagh and Primate of the Catholic Church in Ireland. He was not a natural hero. He was a small, scholarly, introverted man—a large leprechaun, as he once referred to himself. On that Saturday afternoon we locked arms and walked at the head of a procession through a joint Catholic-Protestant area. Protestant young people were jeering at me because I dared to walk with a friend, now a Catholic bishop. We were at that time both doing a bit of teaching at the university.

A person came charging out of a Catholic church, flailing a great crucifix above her head. The person hit Cahal on the back of the head with it, at the same time questioning whether his parents had been married at the time of his birth. She was able to express this idea with a single word. Cahal fell to the ground, blood coming from the back of his head. I asked him if he would like to sit in a shop doorway until we sorted things out. He looked at me with steely eyes, which I shall never forget, and he said 'James, put your hand into my pocket, get out a handkerchief, wipe the back of my head, clean me up, and up we get and on we go'. He was over seventy at the time. He said to me, 'If at this point we fail, if at this point we do not go on, than all those words that we spout from the pulpit will be shown up for the hypocrisy that they are. Community and peace will, under God, come by what we do now.'

3

Living with Difference: Identity and Belonging

Kathy Galloway

A few years ago, I visited Bosnia with a group of British Christians and Muslims. One of the most interesting and challenging aspects of the visit for me was discovering an indigenous, white community that had been Muslim for centuries. They were not migrants or refugees, they were as European as I was, and they shared the same concerns, aspirations and values. It was an important lesson; I realised how many of the assumptions I make about Islam had been shaped by my experience of the Scottish Muslim community, which mostly originated in Pakistan, and how many of these assumptions were primarily cultural rather than religious. It also gave me a renewed sense of the rich diversity of Europe, and how little we appreciate or value it. Though we go to considerable lengths now to protect bio-diversity, we are not so good at engaging with cultural diversity, and European history is somewhat compromised in this regard.

In every country in the world one of the major challenges of the twenty-first century is how we are to live with difference? For indeed, we must find ways to live together in peace, though we are different, because there are no good alternatives. We have seen the way of separation and division; in Northern Ireland, behind the ironically titled 'peace lines'; in the Balkans; in apartheid South Africa, in Israel/Palestine. This is not a good alternative. We have seen the way of ethnic cleansing, of warfare, of genocide. This is an even worse alternative, a many-headed hydra that breeds more death.

We are people of faith, and our vision is of better alternatives. And truly we must increasingly take on responsibility for shaping the world. How shall we live, not fearfully but with the glorious freedom of the children of God? Where are our resources for resistance and persistence in our faith?

I want today to reflect on three stories of biblical women who took on responsibility for shaping the world. The first is a narrative of exile. Ruth is a foreigner in Israel, a lone woman. Her economic situation is precarious in the extreme: seeking to provide for herself and her mother-in-law—an Israelite whose life and faith Ruth has identified with, and whom she has served unstintingly—Ruth goes to glean in the fields of Boaz, Naomi's kinsman. Here, Ruth is at her most vulnerable. Being the people of God obviously does not inhibit the Israelite men from feeling at liberty to molest or abuse a woman alone. After Boaz's kindnesses, Naomi's suggestion for Ruth to sleep at Boaz's feet, is for Ruth's potential good. 'This will bring you security,' says Naomi, sending Ruth to Boaz's bed to trade with her only possession, her own body, knowing that if there is any security to come from it, she, Naomi, will also take a share in it. And if it all goes wrong . . . well, Naomi is spared those consequences; after all, Ruth is a Moabite!

The book of Ruth is often described as a gentle and peaceful one, preceded as it is by the extreme gender violence of the Book of Judges. But it isn't really. Its apparently good ending not only masks the question of what happened to all the other foreign women who did not find a Boaz; it can lead us to overlook what happens to people who are powerless in the face of intransigent social systems.

This is a period in post-exilic Israelite history of vicious legislation against interethnic marriage, of Gentile women and their children summarily divorced and abandoned. Furthermore, Moabite women in particular are stigmatised as sexually promiscuous and idolatrous. And yet this Moabite is in every respect faithful, loving and loyal.

Ruth is exposed, the alien who must prove herself to find even a modicum of acceptance. Above all, Ruth is the supplicant. She must humble herself, must in dependency throw herself on another's mercy, asking for help. The need to be a supplicant has not, of course, disappeared. It is a reality that characterises significant aspects of international relations, especially economic relations; it is the experience of asylum-seekers and refugees; it is still the experience of millions of women across the world, and it seeps into the experience of those whose difference or whose minority status make it almost unavoidable. It is the experience today of Lebanon.

To be a supplicant is something that contemporary western culture finds intolerable, almost the ultimate humiliation, especially but not solely for men. To receive without being able to give in return we find demeaning. Yet even in our culture of power and autonomy, the experience of being a supplicant touches us too: when ageing or illness forces us to relinquish our powers; when unemployment or family crisis or personal injury removes them, or simply when we find ourselves in situations completely beyond our control. Perhaps one of the reasons we are so fearful, almost pathologically so (we who are the powerful of the West), is that minorities, because they have no automatic belonging, must supplicate again and again, confronting us with what we most fear—our own vulnerability, our own lack, our own most deep-seated failure. Far easier to anathematise them, project our fears, distance ourselves. They are the part of ourselves that we cannot bear to confront. And yet they are a part that we need in order to be wholly human.

The story of Ruth, which opens with barrenness and despair, comes to a close with healing, wholeness and hope. This transformation arises through Ruth's resistance and struggle. We see in the outsider the epitome of God's self-giving spirit of reconciliation. She has endured with dignity, and others with and through her have been restored. This is a story to counter the excesses of Ezra's pogrom against foreigners and mixed marriages. It remains defiant whenever God's people give in to our sectarian egos. And whenever God is appropriated by the cruel or indifferent, or used to baptise injustice, Ruth's story is a basis for trusting the promise of God and the defiance of those bound up in God's life.

At the end of the story, Ruth's voice is silenced. We do not hear her voice or even her name spoken. The wedding between Ruth and Boaz hints at a new relationship that includes both Judah and Moab. But perhaps the absence of Ruth in the text is actually recognising the way our prejudice almost automatically reconfigures itself. Is Ruth now assimilated so that she can become invisible as a Moabite? Can attitudes to Moab, to foreigners, remain unchecked now that she is an honorary Israelite? Or is this the test the story finally sets, not just to the Israelites, but to us?

Concern about minorities has been focused recently by the increased number of economic migrants, like Ruth, into Europe. I am a European. I have a British passport. My belonging is unquestioned, rooted in my colour, my nationality, my language and accent, my religion, and the fact that in all these things, I am part of a majority. I do not have to prove that I belong.

This unquestioned belonging is something that many people in Europe are unable to take for granted, even if they were born there. If they are not white, they will frequently be assumed to be foreigners, asylum seekers or refugees, and because of their permanent visibility, they will be assumed to be present in much greater numbers than they actually are. They may speak excellent English or French or German but if their accent is not recognisably 'European', their belonging will not be unquestioned. If they are Muslim, their belonging may be particularly questioned, sometimes in threatening and hostile fashion, and may make them guilty by association. My belonging, as a Christian, on the other hand, has never been questioned as a result of the violence perpetrated by Christian against Christian in Northern Ireland, or by Christian-originated violence in Bosnia, Iraq or anywhere else in the world.

To be part of a minority, especially a visibly or audibly different one, is to always have to prove one's belonging, and to have no signs of proof ever be enough. Previous generations of immigrants to Europe, attempting to belong, to assimilate like Ruth, were met by an unsettling mixture of racism and exploitation of their labour. Their second and third-generation children, perhaps more confident, or more cynical, have called us on our professions of democracy and individual freedoms, and asserted an identity of difference. In this, they are doing what emigrating Europeans have always done, whether that be in the mission and church planting in Africa and South America which accompanied colonialism, or in expatriate enclaves, or in supplanting indigenous cultures altogether to become the unquestioned majority; they have carried their language, culture, religion, politics and economics, and, let us not forget, in some of these places their military capacity, with them to create places where they could feel at home, where they could belong without always having to prove it.

Our attitude to the emigrating Europeans of the past is interesting. We think of them as brave, resourceful, heroic even. We are compassionate towards the plight that led them to leave—the famines, clearances, poverty and destitution—and we sing about the pain of leaving the homeland, the hardships they endured in the new world. And when their descendants return to the old country to visit, we welcome them with open arms and praise their achievements and prosperity: the cities they founded, the businesses they built up, the churches they planted. We believe that they had no alternative but to go, and we are proud of what they did.

How curious then that our attitudes to immigrants into Europe should be so different. Misunderstanding, racism, relentless hostility are daily experiences, and when the many who are Christian attend churches here, they do not always receive the welcome that our faith demands of us. The irony is that we need them as much as they need us—Scotland, for instance, has a declining, ageing population, along with much of Western Europe. We need the youthful energy, new ideas and skills that immigrants bring. The image of the rich countries of the world, securing their own interests and then pulling the drawbridge up behind them—of Fortress Europe—is not a very good advertisement for the much-lauded benefits of democracy, freedom and free trade! But this is how much of the world understands Christianity.

Some years ago, the BBC screened a play on television about refugees coming to Europe. The last scene is vividly etched on my memory. It was of a pristine southern European beach. Up the beach dozens of ragged, exhausted figures, mostly black, were crawling. On a terrace above the beach, elegantly dressed white people drank cocktails and chatted, turning away in horror from the emaciated bodies below them. The impact of the scene was powerful and unforgettable. At the time, I took it as a metaphor; today, of course, we know that this is actually the way many of the dispossessed arrive in Europe. In the United States, people don't come by sea but through the desert. The risks, however, are the same.

From our viewpoint on the terrace looking down at the beach (and many are looking, not just turning their backs) perhaps we need to think more about what it really means for us to welcome people and include them as full participants in our communities and our churches.

This challenge also faced Jesus in the second text concerning women in the Bible. In Matthew 15, Jesus encounters a Canaanite woman. Here is another supplicant, another outsider. But this is not a daughter acting on behalf of her mother, but a mother in despair for her daughter, seeking his intervention for the sick body and spirit of her child. We are most vulnerable through the children we love, and perhaps we supplicate most deeply on their behalf.

The story is one of only two in the gospel in which healing is offered to a Gentile, and at a distance. This Canaanite woman, one of the indigenous and dispossessed people of Israel, is also alone, without a male to give her a name or protection. She seeks Jesus out, addresses him in the most respectful terms, and supplicates him to have mercy on her suffering child. At first Jesus ignores her, then his disciples ask him to send this noisy woman away. But she, like other women in the gospels, is persistent, and her need is great. She enters into dialogue with him, does not dissent from his description of her people as 'dogs', but rather redirects it and appeals to him once again as Lord. She asserts her claim and demonstrates her faith not by protesting the disdainful reference to her ethnic group, but by arguing that both Gentiles and Jews are under the same authority. Still respectful, she turns his metaphor on its head, with an astute and daring response.

Jesus has already demonstrated that religious custom, such as Sabbath observance, should not stand in the way of responding to human need. Now, challenged to see that social conventions should not do so either, his own integrity requires him to recognise the extent of the woman's faith and to re-examine his own mission. He salutes the woman's faith, and answers her entreaty. It is from this point onwards that Jesus understands that he has been sent not only to the people of Israel but also to the Gentiles. The new relationship will henceforth include them.

Once again, the courage, faith and resourcefulness of a Gentile woman, who takes risks and makes herself vulnerable, change the shape of God's mission. We never know the woman's name, only that she was a Canaanite, that she was alone, that she loved her daughter.

In this story, there is a crucial question of integrity. Integrity is the wholeness of something, reminding us of the holiness of God who when asked by Moses for an ID card and a name replied: 'I am who I am. Tell the people that I am has sent you to them.' When we say that a person, or a church, or a nation has integrity surely this is what we mean. I am who I am.

For diversity to have integrity, it can neither mean endless separation of the parts of the body nor the dreaded uniformity. It does mean the consistency of a coherent identity in the love of God. The most fundamental human integrity is that of spirit and body. The struggle to maintain that integrity, the wholeness of personhood, is acute. So much about our world tends toward disintegration. Political oppression and dispossession, acute poverty, violence of every kind, racism, sexism, xenophobia, homophobia, and the impoverishment of the imagination by consumer capitalism are all deeply damaging to bodies and spirits. Yet the worst threat comes, not from these things themselves, but from our internalisation of them; the subtle ways in which they can colonise our inner landscape, make us internalise their definition of who we are, incline us to live out of our fears and not our freedom.

The church has often colluded with this colonisation, has fed our fears in the interest of its own power and forgotten that we are called to share in the glorious freedom of the children of God. The Canaanite woman, like Ruth, has not been colonised. In the face of insult and rejection, she refuses to accept this as the will of God, and confronts Jesus with her utter conviction that he can help her despite all their differences. She is who she is. And in that identity, she is confirmed.

And finally, in the text of John 12, is Mary of Bethany, another beloved disciple. She has been a supplicant before: when she desired to listen to Jesus teaching; when her brother died and she touched Jesus' heart with her weeping. But this time, we see Mary ministering to Jesus. Her anointing is an act of pure extravagance and Judas, protesting, tries to force an either/or division: either one can love Jesus or one can love the poor. But Jesus refutes Judas by affirming the kind of both/and love that Mary has shown. It is perfectly possible to love both: this is a false and ungenerous dichotomy.

This is a very personal story, yet its beauty and intimacy should not blind us to its wider significance. Mary is anointing Jesus for a bitter and untimely death which both accept as the likely outcome of his challenge to the religious authority of Jerusalem and the political authority of Rome. Her declaration for Jesus is offered to him publicly while he still lives. Her loving act makes visible the violence to which Jesus is to be subjected. She is a model of resistance to violence through the love that acts. It is also a participation in Jesus' suffering and death, a mark of identification with Jesus' passion. Mary does for Jesus now what he will do for his disciples later. *We strain to glimpse his mercy-seat, and find him kneeling at our feet.*

Mary anticipates the commandment that Jesus will give his followers. 'Just as I have loved you, you also should love one another.' She models discipleship. It is an open invitation not just to talk about love, as Judas did, but to be the reminder, in our concrete decisions and actions, that if we have not love, we are nothing. The theologian, Kosuke Koyama, writes:

> What is love if it remains invisible and intangible? . . . Grace cannot function in a world of invisibility. Yet, in our world, the rulers try to make invisible 'the alien, the orphan . . . the hungry, thirsty . . . sick and imprisoned'. This is violence . . . The gospel insists on visibility—the emaciated bodies of starved children must remain visible to the world. There is a connection between invisibility and violence. People, because of the dignity of the image of God they embody, must remain seen. Faith, hope and love are not vital except in 'what is seen' . . . Religion seems to raise up the invisible and despise what is visible. But it is the 'see, hear, touch' gospel that can nurture the hope which is free from deception.[1]

This is love, not as sentiment, but as a deep resistance to all that does violence to, demeans or degrades other human beings. It is also about receiving as well as giving. Jesus' acceptance of, and refusal to condemn Mary's gift is also a gift of love. Finally, Jesus himself becomes the supplicant, giving dignity and grace to vulnerability and need. This is the way we are to be with one another, a way grounded firmly on mutual exchange, acceptance and respect for one another in all our difference, our frailty, our unexpressed and unmet need.

---

1. Kosuke Koyama, 'Together on the Way: Rejoice in Hope'. Available at <http://wccx.wcc-coe.org/wcc/assembly/pth3-e.html>. Accessed 13 June 2007, 1–2.

> The rejoicing of a private and exclusive community fails to invite all to hope. That is not the gospel. Hope with all creation and rejoice with all creation! What a far-reaching horizon! This horizon is not a hallucination. For God no one is stranger . . . We cannot love our neighbours unless we are open to being loved by our neighbours. We cannot extend hospitality to strangers unless we accept hospitality from strangers. The gospel upholds this two-way traffic. One-way traffic breeds self-righteousness.[2]

The Scottish poet, Robert Burns, wrote, 'O, wad some poo'er the giftie gie us, tae see ourselves as ithers see us.' And 'Do for others what you would have them do for you,' said Jesus. This is two-way traffic: to see ourselves from the perspective of the other, and to extend to the other the same generosity and kindness that we wish to receive. According to Edgar Pisani 'Removing all traces of racism from our relations means affirming that we are different and that we shall remain different'. Affirming the right of the 'not us' to be different is a huge responsibility, especially when we are in the majority, and have more choice in the matter; minorities often have to make do with the small space for expression of difference assigned to them. And this task is all the more challenging because we also have to discern what differences really are threatening and to resist all efforts to whip up hysteria about the rest. Our freedoms are not at risk in Europe. Our attachment to our own comforts are much more of a threat.

To see ourselves as others see us from the beach, not the terrace, is not comfortable. Racism depends on the dehumanisation of the 'not us'. But it's also learned from the experience of racism. We must resist every effort to scapegoat and stigmatise, to divide into 'us' and 'them'. Racism makes 'human' the least important definition. The gospel makes it the most important.

Ruth was assimilated; the Canaanite woman was affirmed in her difference. These strategies we are familiar with in Europe. But Mary anointed Jesus into identification with the 'not-us', the minority, the supplicants. I want to finish with another story. A couple of months ago, I was in South Africa, visiting a church in the black township of Guguletu with which the Iona Community has a partnership. Its minister studied for a while in Scotland, and there heard a woman member of the Iona Community speak. She told of how,

---

2. Koyama, 'Together on the Way: Rejoice in Hope', 2.

as a child in rural Scotland, some 'traveller' children had come to her school. 'Travellers' are those who used to be known as gypsies, close relatives of the Roma of other parts of Europe, and they attract the same stigma, abuse and discrimination in Scotland. She described how she would stand at the school window, in tears at the sight of these children being bullied, taunted and pushed about. Then one day, she realised that it was not enough to weep. She had to leave her window, go over to where the children were, and stand beside them. My South African friend had been very moved by this story—it had changed his understanding of his own ministry, and turned it into a quite remarkable and unusual one of service to and solidarity with people in his own very poor community living with HIV/AIDS, another group who have experienced much discrimination and prejudice, not least from fellow Christians.

It was for me a vivid demonstration of the 'see, hear, touch' gospel, of the journey from assimilation through multiculturalism to solidarity with the poorest and most vulnerable, which Jesus himself made, and invites us to make too. And it was a great example of how people taking on responsibility to shape the world create ripples that cross boundaries, cross continents and bear witness to a different way of being.

4

Intimations of a Global Ethic:
Ecumenical Ripples in the *Decade to Overcome Violence*

Jonathan Inkpin

> You know, they marched in Berlin, and the Berlin
> Wall fell, they marched in South Africa, and apartheid
> fell. Now we march in Porto Alegre . . . Jesus has no
> arms but yours. Let us end war for Jesus Christ's sake.
> Let us work for justice for Jesus Christ's sake. We won
> against Communism. We won against apartheid. Now
> will we win against war and violence.

Desmond Tutu's rallying words rang powerfully through the night air of downtown Port Alegre in Brazil. Two thousand people from nations across the world had gathered to take part in a candle-lit march for peace during the most recent World Council of Churches' (WCC) Assembly in February 2006. Such a 'river of light' constituted an impressive backdrop to Tutu's rhetoric and a practical demonstration of commitment to the WCC's *Decade to Overcome Violence*. Yet what theological grounds for hope lie behind this and how do they connect with the strivings of others for peace and reconciliation in our ever more globalised but fragile and divided world?

The question of violence and religion came to the fore at the World Council of Churches when it met in 1998, looking back on the twentieth century, that most violent century in history. In response, the WCC pledged itself, between 2001–2010, to a *Decade to Overcome Violence: Churches Seeking Peace and Reconciliation.* That pledge builds upon the many decades of ecumenical endeavour for peace and reconciliation, not least the foundation of the WCC itself, in 1948, out of the ruins of World War 11. It also marks a welcome contemporary recognition amongst many Christians that we need to look again at what leads to peace. For the creation of the *Decade to Overcome Violence* (or DOV) initiative can partly be seen as a contribution to the search for a 'global ethic' in a world torn by renewed religious, as well as political, social, economic and ecological tensions.

Theologically speaking, the idea of a 'global ethic' is associated with Hans Küng, who first promoted the concept in his 1990 book *Projekt Weltethos*.[1] This is based on a fundamental assumption that the world's major religions can make a meaningful contribution to the peace of humankind if they are willing to draw on their shared convictions and common beliefs. For Küng affirmed that, in spite of all their doctrinal differences, the world's major religions are also united in some fundamental moral beliefs and in a shared vision of life in dignity and mutual respect. Hence his much quoted three-fold nostrum that there can be:

- No peace among the nations without peace among the religions.
- No peace among the religions without dialogue between the religions.
- No dialogue between the religions without investigation of the foundations of the religions.

As Küng himself has pointed out, very few documents relating to a global ethic existed when he initially promoted the idea. There were some declarations on human rights, above all the 1948 Declaration of the United Nations, but little or nothing had been written by world organisations on issues of human responsibility, the essential other dimension to human rights. In the face of the continued globalisation of the economy, technology and media, there has however been a 'globalisation of problems', which exacerbates 'the weakness of human rights' without 'an ethical impulse and a motivation to accept responsibilities'.[2] In response, albeit indirectly or unconsciously, there has been a developing search for global solutions to global problems. This is in the spirit of what Küng calls:

> a globalization of ethic: no uniform ethical system ('ethics'),
> but a necessary minimum of shared ethical values, basic

---

1. English version: *Global Responsibility. In Search of a New World* (London: SCM/ New York: Continuum, 1991).
2. Hans Küng, *Global Ethic and Human Responsibilities*, submitted to the High-level Expert Group Meeting on 'Human Rights and Human Responsibilities in the Age of Terrorism', 1–2 April 2005, Santa Clara University. See at <www.scu.edu/ethics /practicing/focusareas/global_ethics/laughlin-lectures/global-ethic-human-responsi bility.html>.

attitudes and criteria ('ethic') to which all regions, nations and interest groups can commit themselves. In other words . . . a common basic human ethic.

Only this, Küng argues, can help overcome the 'crisis of orientation' at the heart of our global tensions.[3]

The theological work of Christian churches in seeking peace and reconciliation, whether under the *Decade to Overcome Violence* (DOV) or by other means, is not focused on the search for a 'global ethic' as such. Rather, for Christians, it is centred on a renewed understanding and proclamation (in word and deed) of the Gospel of Jesus Christ, the Prince of Peace, in whom God has reconciled the world.[4] Yet most Christian thinkers today recognise that this cannot be achieved without, at the very least, greater recognition of the 'other' beyond the Christian community and, where possible, shared participation in addressing the common problems facing humanity. Certainly this lies at the heart of the *Decade to Overcome Violence* initiative, which specifically calls churches, ecumenical organisations, and all people of goodwill:

- To work together for peace, justice, and reconciliation at all levels.
- To embrace creative approaches to peace building which are consonant with the spirit of the gospel.
- To work with local communities, secular movements, and people of other faiths to cultivate a culture of peace.
- To empower people who are oppressed and act in solidarity with all struggling for justice, peace, and the integrity of creation.
- To repent together for our acts of violence and engage in theological reflection to overcome the spirit, logic, and practice of violence.

This challenge has already been taken up in a number of significant ways by churches, and with peoples of other faith and none. Alliances have been built with other global initiatives, such as the co-terminous *UN Decade for a Culture of Peace and Non-violence for the Children of the World*, and collaborations established with many other groups. In particular, the WCC itself has initiated valuable work and reflection through a series of key projects, including: the Ecumenical Accompaniment Programme in Palestine

---

3. Küng, *Global Ethic and Human Responsibilities*.
4. 2 Corinthians 6:16–20.

and Israel; the Impunity, Truth, Justice, and Reconciliation Programme (which has sought to enhance and learn from truth and reconciliation processes across the world); the Peace to the City network (which has encouraged and shared the insights of models of overcoming violence in several key cities in different parts of the world; a Peacebuilding and Disarmament Programme; work on Microdisarmament; work on Overcoming Violence against Women; work by the WCC International Relations Team (including with the UN); Inter-religious Relations and Dialogue; and, critically, a Faith and Order Study Process.[5] Each year of the *Decade* has also seen a focus on a specific area of the world and its issues of violence (such as on Asia in 2005 and Latin America in 2006). Meanwhile, major DOV-related statements of ecumenical concern have been made: such as those by the WCC Assembly in February 2006, on Latin America; the Responsibility to Protect (as distinct from 'Humanitarian Intervention'); Terrorism, Human Rights and Counter-terrorism; Reforming the United Nations; Water for Life; and the Elimination of Nuclear Arms.[6] Such approaches to global violence are then further reflected in national and local ecumenical work. For, as the National Council of Churches in Australia (NCCA) declared in its opposition to the build-up to war in Iraq:

> The NCCA is currently promoting the *Decade to Overcome Violence*, a call to transcend the 'logic' of violence and find constructive alternatives to war and injustice. The way to peace does not lie through war, but through transforming structures of injustice and the politics of exclusion.

Perhaps most significantly of all, in terms of a 'global ethic', inter-religious dialogue on the hidden connections between religion and violence has become one of the foci of the *Decade*.[7] As the WCC itself observes:

> by its very nature, inter-religious dialogue is not an instrument to resolve problems instantly in emergency situations'. However, the trust that has been built through

5.	For more information see the WCC DOV website <www.overcomingviolence.org>.
6.	WCC DOV website <www.overcomingviolence.org>.
7.	WCC, *Mid-Term of the Ecumenical Decade to Overcome Violence 2001–2010: Churches Seeking Reconciliation and Peace* (Geneva: WCC Assembly document, 2006), 4 available at <www.wcc-assembly.info/fileadmin/files/wccassembly /documents>.

patient dialogue and practical cooperation for the common good 'may in times of conflict prevent religion from being used as a weapon'.[8]

To the theological intimations of this hope let us now turn.

Four ways into overcoming violence, singing *kyrie eleison*

In order to stimulate reflection and action around the *Decade to Overcome Violence*, four major themes have been promoted by the WCC as root causes of violence:

- the spirit and 'logic' of violence;
- the use, abuse and misuse of power;
- issues of justice;
- religious identity and plurality.[9]

These were not idly chosen but were the result of worldwide consultation among churches between 2000–2001 and, as such, they offer more than a scaffolding for the DOV itself. For they lay out an agenda for investigation for all who seek to explore the possibilities of a global ethic or spirit for our age. Such themes are common to human struggle and are both illuminated and frustrated by the practice of the great religions. In addressing this in Australia, for instance, the NCCA has attempted to take up the four key themes by relating them to their foundations in scripture and Christian tradition as expressed in the four great spiritual words of Truth, Mercy, Justice and Community (understood as *koinonia*), and thus seeking to: 'transcend the spirit and logic of violence' (Truth); 'spread power and forgiveness' (Mercy); 'do justice to all' (Justice) and 'grow communities which value diversity' (Community).[10] As such, this process is one which is open to others too. Indeed, in Australia, the choice of the words Truth, Mercy, Justice and Community were made deliberately to be able to resonate with other faith and non-faith perspectives. Not that this implies a lack of complexity or an easy syncretism, but very much the reverse. To address those four key themes

---

8. WCC, *Mid-Term*, quoting *Ecumenical Considerations for Dialogue and Relations with People of Other Religions* (Geneva: WCC, 2003), 12.

9. WCC, *Why Violence? Why Not Peace?* (Geneva: WCC, 2002), 5.

10. See further: <www.ncca.org.au/dov>.

requires close and dedicated attention to the particularities of the great religious traditions. For the task is not that of a religious 'striptease', in which we give away the unique clothing of our faith traditions. Rather the opposite: we need all the resources we can find, religious or otherwise, for our common search for peace. Yet there is also an urgent need to reconsider what part our respective religions play in cultivating peace or facilitating violence.

Reflection on the interconnections of religion and violence thus drive us deeper into the theological and religious task, beginning with an unmasking and letting go of what contributes to violence within religious life and theological debate. 'First and foremost, the *kyrie eleison* must be sung', as the WCC Faith and Order team put it, in their invitation to the process of theological study and reflection on peace, justice and reconciliation during the *Decade to Overcome Violence*. The product of a core group, consisting of leading ecumenical theologians from across the world, this invitation (*Nurturing Peace, Overcoming Violence: In the Way of Christ for the Sake of the World*) lays out key questions for consideration. At its heart however is a call to repentance for complicity in violence and apathy in resistance. DOV, it is insisted, 'is a statement of confession as much as a commitment to a task'.[11]

Truth: transcending the spirit and 'logic' of violence

In outlining the theological insights of the ecumenical *Decade to Overcome Violence*, the preeminent challenge is then for a change of consciousness, not least in the area of truth and truth-telling. This is the core of peace. 'The truth', said Jesus, 'will set you free. Repent (turn around—face the right direction).' Becoming an effective peacemaker involves knowing the truth and standing for it no matter what. All the great peacemakers have shown this. *Satyaghara* (soul force, truth-telling), Gandhi called it and with it he humbled the British Empire. For Gandhi, truth-telling also involved recognising that violence can never be transformed by violence. Rather, as Martin Luther King said, violence is a vicious circle. Yet we persist in it, as if darkness could extinguish darkness. For the spirit and 'logic' of violence appears inexorable. Reflecting on the experience of the first few years of the twenty-first century, 'strengthening the spirituality of non-violence' has thus been highlighted as

---

11. Faith and Order Team, *Nurturing Peace, Overcoming Violence: In the way of Christ for the sake of the World* (Geneva: WCC 2003), available at <www.oikoumene.org/en/resources/documents/wcc-commissions/faith-and-order-commission>.

one of the key areas of concern in this second half of the *Decade*. In the words
of the DOV Mid-Term report:

> the first half of the *Decade* was overshadowed by brutal acts
> of international terrorism and the reactions to it . . . Seldom
> before have the spirit, logic and practice of violence
> manifested themselves so openly. The challenge to the
> churches to relinquish any theological and ethical
> justification of violence calls for the exercise of spiritual
> discernment that draws its strength from a spirituality of
> active non-violence. Here the churches are in need of mutual
> support and encouragement.[12]

A number of critical theological doctrines therefore need to be further
addressed by theologians in assisting the churches in their witness to the
nonviolence of Jesus and in offering their distinctive contribution to a 'global
ethic'. As the DOV invitation to theological study suggests, these include: the
influence of some doctrines of creation, fall and human being on churches'
attitudes towards racism, sexual discrimination, social hierarchies, the
suppression of human freedom and subjugation of the powerless; the way
doctrines of atonement can legitimise the suffering of the innocent; Christian
triumphalism that has left continuing memories of violence; certain biblical
trajectories which hold violence as a divine attribute; attempts towards
enculturation which sometimes ignore the oppressive potential of certain
dominant cultures; evangelisation strategies which allow silence or neutrality
in situations of great injustice; concepts of peace as inner tranquillity or
absence of conflict which trivialise violence, forgiveness and reconciliation;
traditional forms of *diakonia* which limit Christian responses to binding the
wounds of victims; and the failure to internalise the values of justice and
peace in the ways in which churches pursue their ecclesial existence,
sometimes exacerbated by denominational loyalties in situations of
brokenness.[13]

Such a weighty agenda is thoroughly testing but is the substance of the
kyrie eleison which the churches are called to sing if Christians are truly
serious about addressing religious complicity with violence. Certainly,
without naming the truth of what has gone *before,* we cannot have any real

---

12. See further: <www.ncca.org.au/dov>, 4.

13. WCC, *Mid-Term*, 5.

peace. That is at the core of the truth and reconciliation processes which, beginning in South Africa with Desmond Tutu, have sought to heal the underlying pain which needs addressing, even when there is surface resolution. Can we hear one another's pain and not recoil? Can we offer one another forgiveness and apology? In some cases religious leaders have wisely begun to do so, notably for example, in papal apologies for Christian involvement in such horrors as the medieval Crusades and the Holocaust. Yet there is much more to be done across the religious spectrum, as we see in the continued lack of acknowledgement of the past experience of others, whether, for example, in the traumas of the Middle East, the tribulations of the Armenian and many Asian peoples, or the sufferings of the Indigenous. As the varied experience of truth and reconciliation processes has shown, where ever truth is hidden or only partially disclosed, little of genuine, lasting, significance can be achieved. Can we be truthful about our histories?

Can we be truthful also, about the way our religious texts themselves have been used, and are still used, by some, to justify violence? That is a hard call. Within Australia itself, we have seen how faith groups can be acutely sensitive to remarks by others, such as those, for instance, by Cardinal Pell on aspects of the *Qur'an*. This is often so, even where, as in the Cardinal's case, the commentator has a clear and deep commitment to inter-religious dialogue. It may be difficult for outsiders to comment without causing offence or reaction. Yet, if so, there is all the more need for those of us *within* our own particular faith traditions to be truthful about what helps and what hinders. This is not about cutting bits out of our sacred texts, as if we were able to be God rewriting them. A politically-correct, anaemic Bible is not a helpful aim. It is often the most difficult passages that really help us, if we are willing to wrestle with them. Yet we must be truthful that there are some aspects of our faiths which *can* become 'texts of terror': if, that is, we take them selectively from the whole, and apart from the love that underpins the whole. As the case of Sheikh Al-Hilaly, the Mufti of Australia, shows, without such attention religious and secular passions are much more likely to be enflamed rather than appropriately directed.

The continuing proliferation of inter-religious dialogues at various levels offers considerable hope for a greater understanding of the spirit and truth of violence and for the development of a 'global ethic'. Yet this is not without considerable theological challenge. As Hans Ucko, of the WCC Inter-religious Relations and Dialogue team, has expressed it, 'one runs almost as if by design into one issue: the interrelationship between the question of truth, our faith claims, the faith claims of others and how to deal with religious plurality'.[14] This issue will be considered further below, in relation to 'growing communities which value diversity'. For the moment, it is important to note that genuine inter-religious dialogue is neither a process of defining our religions by their ideals, nor (as Hans Ucko puts it) simply an ambulance to solve the conflicts that rage around us. Instead, as members of the WCC 'Thinking Together' process early in the *Decade to Overcome Violence* affirmed, the search for truth, though grounded in past history and revelation, is self-critical, future-orientated and outward looking:

> We, members of five religious traditions—Buddhism, Christianity, Hinduism, Islam and Judaism—came together with deep concern about the growing violence in the world today. Our own traditions give us our ethical values and offer us a vision of peaceful co-existence predicated upon justice and harmony with the earth. We are conscious of the need to be self-critical and to go beyond a discourse shaped by narrow political, national, economic or military objectives. We endeavour to go beyond religious idealism and explore concrete modes of expression and action.[15]

The 'Thinking Together' process has been but one element in the attempts of ecumenical movement to seek truth with others and thereby address the first key DOV theme of the spirit and 'logic' of violence. Many of its concerns highlight however the continued challenge to religious thinkers: the realities of our contemporary world which find religions actively engaged in violence and which call religions to a re-evaluation of their concepts (such as the Christian doctrine of 'just war'); the importance of clarifying terminology (not least that of '*jihad*' in Islam); the 'mixed messages' and problematic images of God (such as the warrior God) presented by sacred texts; the importance of seeing texts in their original context and in the context and pressures of the

---

14. 'Truth and Truths', *Current Dialogue*, Issue 37, June 2001, (WCC), available at <www.wcc-coe.org/wcc/what/interreligious/cd37-09.html>.

15. *Religion and Violence: Message of the Participants* (WCC Conference, Eckerd College, St Petersburg, Florida, 8–12 February 2002), available at <www.wcc-coe.org/wcc/what/interreligious/cd39-08.html>.

contemporary world; and the assumptions about how to view humanity (and particularly humanity beyond the religious group) which religions inculcate.[16]

Fundamentally, the ecumenical search to transform the spirit and logic of violence is also underpinned by the strong conviction that truth is relational. In the words of one Catholic writer:

> I believe that, for most of us today, it is friendship that transforms our commitment of justice from work for a cause to a way of life. Until you have a friend who is poor, poverty remains an issue that you can walk away from at any time. Only when you have a friend who has been violated, can you lose the clinical distance which makes debates about good violence and bad violence seem reasonable. Until you have a friend who is a refugee, you do not factor in the human cost of war. Your friend is the one who faces you, who summons you to face yourself. Your friend is the angel of the annunciation summoning you to remain life-size in a time of moral diminishment.[17]

Mercy: spreading power and forgiveness

The importance of relationship in the search for the truth about violence and its transformation is intimately related to the associated necessity of mercy-power, or active compassion. As one of four thematic foci of the *Decade to Overcome Violence*, a deeper theological understanding of 'the use, abuse and misuse of power', and the way out of it, is clearly critical. For this reason, the ecumenical invitation to theological reflection (*Nurturing Peace, Overcoming Violence*) calls for an 'interrogation of power', including seeking 'alternative paradigms' which urgently 'redefine power as a divine gift to "do good and to seek justice and peace"'.[18]

As part of its own theological commitment, the WCC has facilitated a series of consultations and conferences on the subject of power, and its use, abuse and misuse in contemporary situations of violence. Such a theological discourse is also recognised as vital in a range of continuing ecumenical

16. Tikva Frymer-Kensky, 'Religions and Violence: An Analytical Synthesis', *Current Dialogue*, Issue 37, June 2001, (WCC).
17. Mary Jo Leddy, 'Romero and John Paul II: Now They See Face to Face', *National Catholic Reporter*, April 5, 2005.
18. Frymer-Kensky, 'Religions and Violence, 3–4.

activities, including in the areas of church and mission, the ministry of ordination, theological anthropology, ethnicity, nationalism and the unity and purpose of the church, as well as on social, economic and political questions such as the work of the UN, economic globalisation, climate change and violence against women. Much could be said on each of these. For the moment however, due to the breadth of these concerns, it is enough to highlight some common major themes.

Firstly, there is a recognition that a new public theology of power is required. For the continuing process of globalisation has changed the concentrations of power and assisted the erosion of traditional power centres, including received notions of sovereignty and the role of the state. As the former WCC general secretary, Konrad Raiser has pointed out, the issue of power has been at the heart of much ecumenical endeavour. Initially, in the genesis of the WCC, the major concern was around the power of the state. Totalitarian rule was in the limelight and definitions of the 'responsible society' were proposed. After this, ecumenical ethical discussion shifted to interpreting 'rapid social change', recognising the rise of new technologies which affected the power of government and others. Affirmations of the reality of 'people's power' resulted. Then came a third phase of ecumenical discourse on power, centred on the notion of a 'just, participatory and sustainable society', which led to fresh affirmations of the nature of power as accountable to God. Today, the context of globalisation and the question of the legitimacy of new forms of distribution of power demand fresh theological attention.[19]

The consequence, say many voices in the ecumenical movement, is that new theological reflection concerning power should be grounded in the experience of the global 'south'. As theologians from the 'south' have constantly remarked, their common experience is a continuing destruction of their people, communities, and environment resulting from the past and persistent colonisation of their countries by others. The need to name and interrogate the 'empire' of oppression (in its various guises and effects) is therefore paramount. For such thinkers, the central subject matters of theology must therefore be issues such as neo-liberal economic globalisation, the war

---

19. WCC Commission on Faith and Order, *Interrogating and Redefining Power: A Theological Consultation* (Geneva: WCC, May 2004), 2–3.

on terror, pre-emptive wars, militarisation, increasing poverty amongst the poor, and religious fundamentalism.[20]

Such privileging of the 'south', as 'the hub of experience of the empire's destructive potential as well as its resistance to it',[21] needs balancing with the recognition also of the fragmented nature of Christianity in the 'south' and the negative aspects of cultural life or traditional Christianity present within it. In addition to fresh courage and solidarity, effective mercy-power for the poor and the powerless of the world requires recognition and healing of the brokenness and limitations of traditional cultures and resistance movements. This is particularly the case when consideration of the (re)imaging of God is raised. Theologians from the 'south' have frequently pointed out the way in which womanist/feminist and many people-based theologies have offered creative possibilities to re-image God as a 'a gracious God' rather an a 'powerful God' (in conventional terms).[22] Such theological investigation can offer fresh models of power which are more life-affirming and ethically responsible. Yet not all models are appropriate to every situation and all such conceptions and structures stand under the 'ideological suspicion' of God. Interrogating and redefining power thus challenge the churches to reflect further on their own use of power, both in terms of specific language and imagery and also in how the power of interpretation is used.

A major inference drawn by the WCC is that, in the second half of the *Decade to Overcome Violence*, 'the churches should be encouraged continuously to open themselves even more deliberately in their witness and service to become "ambassadors of reconciliation" (2 Cor 5)'. This practical outflowing of mercy-power would involve offering responsible accompaniment and support for projects initiated at the grassroots, and, in particular, affirming much more publicly and forcefully the building up of structures and means of non-violent civilian conflict management; and promoting a civilian and non-violent understanding of security.[23] To put the gospel of reconciliation into practice in this way is to demonstrate Jesus' power of service as an alternative

---

20. See also: WCC Commission on Faith and Order, *Interrogating and Redefining Power: Consultation of Younger Theologians from the South* (Chainag Mai, 23–28 February 2004), 1.
21. WCC Commission on Faith and Order, *Interrogating and Redefining Power: A Theological Consultation*, 3.
22. WCC Commission on Faith and Order, *Interrogating and Redefining Power: A Theological Consultation*, 4.
23. WCC, *Mid-Term*, 8.

model to the power of domination (as seen in Mark 10:35–45). By becoming more inclusive, relational communities, and sharing more fully in Jesus' identification with the weakest, most despised, and excluded, churches then hold greater potential as sources of resurrection life.

Justice

Can the churches 'live in the truth' as sources of mercy-power? The ecumenical hope of the *Decade* is assuredly that the churches may be strengthened to affirm human dignity, the rights of people and the integrity of creation. This requires attention to issues of justice. The connections are clear. As the WCC Mid-Term report observes, in words very relevant to the Australian journey of reconciliation:

> In the context of the many 'truth commissions', attention has been drawn to the intimate relationship that exists between reconciliation and the uncovering of truth . . . advocacy for truth and resistance against its distortion have to be considered as an important response . . . (and) no solution of conflict or even process of reconciliation is possible without the participation of the people concerned . . . The *Decade* should strengthen the readiness and courage of the churches 'to live in the truth', even where this places them in opposition to the prevailing political power interests, and thus to open ways towards reconciliation.[24]

In Australia, the National Council of Churches has sought to highlight justice for Indigenous people as the baseline of its DOV commitment, above all through the 'Make *Indigenous* Poverty History' campaign launched by the National Aboriginal and Torres Strait Islander Ecumenical Commission.[25] This rests on the understanding that injustice is indeed one of the root causes of violence. As the Reverend Shayne Blackman has rightly observed:

> It was once said by Mahatma Gandhi that poverty is the worst form of violence. I would like to add that poverty is also the worst form of terrorism. We as Indigenous

---

24. WCC, *Mid-Term*, 7–8.
25. See further: <www.ncca.org.au/natsiec/miph>.

> Australians have unceremoniously experienced the worst
> form of terrorism . . . while violence perpetuated through
> terrorism is deplorable, I would draw your attention to the
> violence at home: violence you will rarely see on any media,
> nor a violence perpetuated through terrorism or civil acts of
> war but a violence of the spirit, body and mind; a violence
> perpetuated through poverty.[26]

Blackman's call to 'restore shalom' is one that expresses well the nature both
of the DOV challenge and the search for a 'global ethic'. Key to this is the
promotion of alternative human visions of security, based on religious insight
and tradition. For, as the DOV Mid-Term report commented:

> The concern for security has become the dominant motif for
> individual as well as social and political decisions. More and
> more, traditional approaches based on the notion of national
> security and its defence by military means seem to be gaining
> the upper hand once again . . . The notion of human security
> as being safe at home and in the community deserves more
> attention and education.[27]

As an adjunct, and 'decisive contribution' to the DOV, the ecumenical
movement has consequently been charged with exploring an *'Alternative
Globalisation Addressing Peoples and Earth'* (AGAPE).

In addition to such engagement with issues of economic injustice,
globalisation and security, two other concerns have also come to the fore. The
first of these is militarisation, the complementary opposite to the spirituality of
nonviolence for which the DOV calls. Again this is linked to the tightly
limited notion of security, based on certain national and military interests,
which has facilitated significant arms proliferation and a growth in the general
militarisation of the world, after a short period of actual disarmament in all
categories of weapons.[28] The second concern is the need for an adequate
doctrine of 'just peace' in response. This notion has appeared more and more

---

26. Speech at the National Aboriginal and Torres Strait Islander Ecumenical
    Commission, 'Hearts are Burning' Forum, Townsville, 2005, full text at
    <www.ncca.org.au/natsiec/theology/light_of_australia/restoring_a_shalom>.
27. WCC, *Mid-Term*, 4–5.
28. WCC, *Mid-Term*, 5

frequently in ecumenical discourse, in contrast to continuing questioning of 'just war' theory in the contemporary context. A number of helpful contributions have been made, including the development of the concept of the 'responsibility to protect' (out of shared unease about the juxtaposition of 'humanitarian' and 'intervention') and the promotion of active non-violence strategies. Yet, as the WCC DOV observes: 'no convincing foundation or action-oriented practical implementation has so far been developed . . . what are the minimum requirements that must be fulfilled with regard to human security and the respect for the rights and dignity of people in order to be able to speak of peace?'[29]

Community of unity in diversity: growing relationships which value religious identity and plurality

As indicated above, the recognition of religious identity and plurality is certainly foundational for DOV and for the pursuit of a 'global ethic'. Partly this is reactive. For the use of religious loyalties connected with ethnic identity is regularly mobilised in order to legitimise situations of violent power conflicts. Beyond being an 'ambulance' however, there is a growing sense that, in this period of the *Decade to Overcome Violence*, we are called 'to discover afresh the meaning of sharing a common humanity'.[30]

The ecumenical commitment to inter-religious dialogue is firmly grounded in the distinctive Christian doctrine of God as Holy Trinity, a community of love, in which each person of the Godhead is different yet equal, bound together in inextricable unity through the power of mutual love. As the DOV Mid-Term report expresses it, this is an 'image for reconciled living':

> The ecumenical fellowship of churches strongly manifests the conviction that the communion of all saints, which is a gift from God and rooted in God's triune life, can overcome the culture of enmity and exclusion which continuously leads into the vicious circles of violence.[31]

---

29. WCC, *Mid-Term*, 6.
30. Hans Ucko, 'Introduction to the "Thinking Together"', group consultation, *Current Dialogue*, Issue 37, June 2002 (WCC).
31. WCC, *Mid-Term*, 9.

Such affirmations build on the long history of ecumenical reflection on the nature of difference and of *koinonia*. In the contemporary context they need however to be re-thought in dialogue with others who do not share the same foundational understanding of God. This has been, and continues to be the most painful theological and spiritual task, beyond that of cultivating compassion or mobilising justice. For how are we, as Hans Ucko asks, to relate 'Truth', as understood in our religious confessions, to the truths of others? Ucko himself posits a form of what we may call 'committed pluralism', pointing back to earlier ecumenical attempts to engage with the issue, including the overlooked Baar Declaration of 1990 on 'Religious Plurality: Theological Perspectives and Affirmations.' Such a stance, he contends, 'does not mean that we concede to indifferentism, saying that everything is relative or an illusion.' This would be to make an absolute of the relative, and, by making no room for commitment, undermine the basis of religious life.[32] Yet, the search for truth must be different in our times from the singular, unitary, univocal talk of the past. Globalisation itself 'is a process of universalisation of a value system' and no religion can simply withdraw as an island unto itself. In contrast, 'an affirmation of diversity is a counter witness to universalisation.'[33]

It is perhaps at this stretching point that real progress in the search for a 'global ethic' is made, towards an ethic which reflects the intricate mosaic of religious bio-diversity. Whilst hardly an easy path, there are signs that steps can be taken together. The limits for such fellow travelling are pressing. To what extent, for example, can values, even when regarded as common, be separated from their significance within the wholeness of each religious tradition?[34] Is inter-religious dialogue condemned always to be essentially descriptive rather than re-creative? The very concept of a 'global ethic' is also problematic if it becomes another form of Western universalisms or obscures the commitment to a genuine search for truth which respects the particularity of revelation, culture, context and experience. Yet there are intimations of a less bleak prognosis. Within Christian-Muslim dialogues for example, there is a growing awareness that a shared and indispensable contribution can be made to affirming that the principles of human rights and religious freedom, despite

---

32. Ucko, 'Introduction to the "Thinking Together"', 4.
33. Ucko, 'Introduction to the "Thinking Together"', 4.
34. *International and Global Inter-religious Initiatives: Reflections from a WCC Consultation,* Hong Kong, 8-12 April 2002, available at <www.wcc-coe.org/wcc/what/interreligious/cd39-15.html>.

the examples of this being honoured in the breach by Christians and Muslims in the past and present.[35] Truth, Mercy, Justice and Community are religious themes to which different religious groups can offer constructive contributions to a larger whole. As the creators of the Arab Muslim-Christian Covenant, adopted in Cairo in December 2001, challenged their co-religionists:

> We urge religious scholars, people of culture and the
> intelligentsia of both Islam and Christianity to seek out the
> common spiritual and humanitarian values in the heritage of
> both religions and in the life-styles of their adherents. We
> urge them to highlight the positive and bright examples of
> how people can live together, stand in solidarity with each
> other, express mutual respect, and show each other affection.
> This will enliven the broad spectrum of society with the
> spirit of dialogue and tolerance in public life. Wisdom is
> what believers always seek, and they are called to assess
> things using the measure of justice and honest scales, not
> debasing the things of others.[36]

Conclusion: a river of light or ripples of peace?

It could be argued that, like Desmond Tutu's speech in Porte Alegre, the concept of a 'global ethic' itself is too prophetic or sanguine, or both. Similarly, it may be contended that the *Decade to Overcome Violence* is also overly ambitious. Nonetheless its key themes go to the roots of much of the violence in which religion is implicated today. For ultimately DOV is a spiritual and theological challenge, first and foremost to the churches themselves. In the long term, as the WCC itself observes, the DOV 'will be judged by whether it will have led to a change of consciousness and to deepened insights into the theological, ethical and spiritual foundations of Christian action for peace'. Can it become 'a river of light'?

If not a river in full flood, the DOV, like the concept of a 'global ethic' may at least inspire deeper consideration of the religious elements which are thrown into the pool of life. For, as Uncle Bob Randall, Aboriginal elder from Central Australia, opines, in a complementary image which resonates strongly

---

35. WCC, *Striving Together in Dialogue: A Muslim-Christian Call to Reflection and Action* (Routledge, 2001) 5.
36. '*Dialogue and Coexistence1*': *An Arab Muslim-Christian Covenant* (WCC, 2001), 5.

with the wider Australian attempts to engage with the *Decade to Overcome Violence*:

> Spirituality is the ultimate answer to reconciliation in Australia and everywhere else in the world. Loving ourselves, our families, our neighbours, our country and every living thing is the reason we are here on earth. If we follow the ripple in the pond where a stone hits the water, we can easily see that the entire pond is affected by that one little stone. If the stone represents love, and it drops somewhere in our universe, that love will send its ripple throughout the entire universe . . . It is the same with anger and hate. We must choose which ripples we wish to send into our universe.[37]

---

37. Bob Randall, *Songman: The Story of an Aboriginal Elder* (Sydney: ABC, 2003), 242.

5

The Road to Justice in Indonesia: Restorative Justice in *Islah*, the Tribunal and the Truth and Reconciliation Commission

Mohammad Iqbal Ahnaf

Introduction

Suharto's presidential era, the authoritarian 'New Order' (*Orde Baru*), was one of the most violent regimes in the world. More than one million people were killed in attempts to maintain the regime's power. Supported by the army, the bureaucracy and capital interests, the regime created a militaristic system that applied repressive policies to any opposition. The long list of New Order violence started from the outset of its power in 1965 and lasted beyond its demise in 1998. Well-known cases of the regime's violence include the mass killings of hundreds of people suspected of being members of the communist party in 1965; the massacre of civilians during military operations in Aceh; the murder of Muslim activists during the Komando events in 1980; and the killing of civilians in East Timor, Papua, Tanjung Priok, Lampung and Jakarta. The violence of the New Order was not only in the form of mass killing, but also in kidnappings, disappearances, torture and rape. The violence had, and still has, serious consequences for the victims and their families and friends. These include trauma, loss of property and economic resources and the on-going stigmatisation of being labeled a communist, rebel or extremist.

With the transition of power from Suharto in 1998 the new government was left with the consequences of the New Order's human right violations. This was inevitably a great burden for the new government. Victims, their families and the general public were not hopeful that truth would be able to emerge and had little hope in the possibility of opening cases involving New Order violence. With Abdurrahman Wahid's presidency in 1999 came the first attempts to systematically address the human rights violations inflicted during the New Order regime. In 2000 the Indonesian House of Representative (DPR) provided two possibilities for addressing gross human rights violations: an ad-hoc tribunal and the Truth and Reconciliation Commission (TRC). Ad-hoc tribunals had already been operating; however, the TRC is still to be made functional. This is because supporting laws are still being discussed in the DPR, a slow process due to the struggle between the interests of the on-going supporters of the New Order and those wanting reform in Indonesian politics.

Although most victims prefer a legal process through the ad-hoc tribunal, this has not yet provided much hope of bringing the elites of the New Order and military to the court. Victims, their families and communities must still wait for justice. Because of several serious barriers within the Indonesian system there is a general scepticism towards the notion of addressing the human rights violations of the New Order through the legal processes.

The political transition from the militaristic and repressive regime of the New Order to a reformist government was not a clean break with the past. Within the reformist government there are still representatives who were also a part of the (old) New Order. This situation in Indonesia makes it very different to that of South Africa, where the government experienced a total change of personnel when the new non-apartheid government took power from the old apartheid regime. In South Africa it was clear as to who were the offenders. In Indonesia, although for many people it is clear that it was the military under the control of the New Order who was the perpetrator of many human rights violations, there is a great complexity concerning evidence and procedural issues. From the many cases of gross human rights violation, few of them have proceeded to the tribunal, and from the few cases that went to the tribunal the outcomes still do not meet the victims' and the community's sense of justice. The legal process could not bring the army generals and the elites of the New Order to the court, including the main perpetrator, the ex-president, Suharto. Instead, it only brought to trial those in the lower ranks, carrying out the orders in the field. The military and elites of the New Order have never been willing to admit their wrongdoings in the past. They have always argued that what they have done was to defend the security and unity of the Republic of Indonesia. They have argued that every human rights violation was a case of a procedural mistake in the field.

The New Order still has powerful representatives not just within the political system, but also within the military, the judicial system and the economy. This presents huge dilemmas for the process of addressing the past violations. The new government sees the uncovering of the truth, due legal process, and the need for personal and societal justice as important. However there is also the fear that such a process will create national disintegration and mayhem. In the past, the face of the New Order was not simply repressive. While they exploited Indonesian economic resources for a group of elites and applied repressive measures to its opponents, they also offered prosperity for opportunists who supported the regime. The number of those who enjoyed the 'cake' from the New Order is not insignificant. And those who benefited still have powerful lobbies in politics (through the *Golkar* and PKPB parties), in the economy (through business interests of the Suharto conglomeration), and within the military (the conservative wing of the army). Understandably, those who benefited from the New Order are still very loyal to its elites and to the military and they use their power to defend the elites in the legal process.

The attempts to protect the New Order elites were not only made through the legal and political processes, but also through policies of terror. An example of the use of terror was the Christian-Muslim conflict in Maluku Island. There is a strong indication that elements of the New Order and the military engineered the Maluku conflict. They did this in an attempt to bargain with the new government to discontinue any policy that harmed the elites of the New Order and the military. This was particularly concerned with the attempts of the new government to bring army soldiers and corrupt businessmen connected to Suharto's businesses to the court. Elites of the New Order were worried that any legal process would result in the uncovering of their past crimes.

Islah: Reconciliation without the pursuit of truth and moral judgment

Because of the barriers and pitfalls involved in these formal processes seeking truth and justice, people turned to an informal, Islamic solution to the problems. *Islah*, an Arabic term meaning 'peace settlement', was initiated in the case of the Tanjung Priok incident. Tanjung Priok is a poor area in South Jakarta. In 1984 Muslim activists from the area held a rally to protest against *Pancasila* (the five pillars of Indonesian identity, based on a universal, humanistic democracy) as the sole ideology of Indonesia and demanded the use of Islam as the base for its social or political organisations. A platoon of military blocked the rally and resorted to indiscriminate shooting, which killed more than thirty-three people. (The estimate of deaths ranges from the official nine to several hundred.) Through the process of *Islah*, seven people—who represented the victims of the Tanjung Priok shooting incidents—met with seven soldiers who were convicted perpetrators of the incident.

The incident had been already been the subject of several processes. The Indonesian National Commission of Human Rights identified thirty-three people who were to be held accountable, including Generals Benny Moerdani and Try Sutrisno. Following the pattern of holding only those in the lower ranks accountable, the ad hoc human rights tribunal indicted fourteen personnel but this did not include those two generals. It also acquitted Special Forces (*Kopassus*) Commander Major General Sriyanto of any responsibility, though he as a captain led the platoon of soldiers who shot at the protesters in Tanjung Priok. He later became Chief of the North Jakarta Military District Operations. The tribunal also acquitted Major General (retired) Pranowo, who was then POM commander in Jakarta.[1]

Toward the end of the ad-hoc tribunal process Try Sutrisno and Benny Moerdani, facilitated by two respected Indonesian Muslim intellectuals, Nurcholish Madjid and Sholahuddin Wahid, initiated *Islah*. Both parties saw that *Islah* was not an alternative to a legal solution. Rather, they saw it as an Islamic solution which involved a sacred agreement based on both parties willingness to find an eternal religious solution.[2] The victims of the Tanjung Priok tragedy said that they accepted *Islah* because they were tired of waiting for the long and unpromising legal process and were wary of the tendency in politicians to serve their own political agenda while pretending to defend them. They had expected the case to be closed as both sides had agreed through the *Islah* to put the past behind them. Though the *Islah* was an informal process, it obviously influenced the legal processes that were to follow. Many victims who had participated in the *Islah* changed their testimonies. It may have been because of these changes of testimonies that Major Generals Sriyanto and Pranowo were finally released.

Interestingly, *Islah* seemed to be beneficial to both the victims and offenders. It was restorative because it helped to heal the wounds of the victims and restored relationships between victims and offenders. This restoration was obvious from the victims' expression of happiness and satisfaction at the outcome of the *Islah*. After the *Islah*, a victim of the Tanjung Priok tragedy said that the result of *Islah* gave him and other victims a sense of brotherhood, a form of concrete honesty that solved all the until then unsolvable problems. During later ad-hoc tribunal processes, which brought Sriyanto and Pranowo as the accused, many victims had placards saying, '*Islah* = Our Happiness'. After Pranowo and Sriyanto were released,

1. Urip Hudiyono, 'Court to Grill upon Reconciliation', *The Jakarta Post*, 5 January 2004.
2. Iwan, '*Try Tentang Kasus HAM Tanjung Priok*', *Kompas*, 22 March 2001.

they also expressed their satisfaction and confirmed the judge's decision saying that they were not involved in the incidents.[3]

What made *Islah* restorative for the victims? I could not find information that gives a detailed description of the *Islah* process. However, it was clear that *Islah* resulted in restitution. Victims admitted that, although restitution was not discussed during the *Islah* process, they received money from officials in the military ranging from two to thirty million Indonesian rupiah. They also admitted that the Penerus Bangsa Foundation had committed to give them employment.[4] The influence of *Islah* in changing the testimonies of the victims so that they favoured the accused also suggests a plea bargain in the *Islah* process. The army would pay restitution and find the victims employment if they would change their testimonies. However, due to my limited comprehension of the *Islah* process, I cannot say that this was the only thing that made the *Islah* work restoratively. Religious motivation, the personal charisma of the facilitators, Nurcholish Madjid and Sholahuddin Wahid, and disillusionments with the legal processes could also have been contributing factors in changing the victims' perceptions of justice.

The *Islah* process did not pursue truth and moral judgment, two elements which are usually essential in any restorative justice yardstick. Through the lens of restorative justice, information concerning the truth-telling of what actually happened, and why something bad happened to the victims is seen as important to healing. It requires a moral judgment that denounces the wrongdoing and recognises the suffering inflicted on the victims. It would seem that these elements did not occur in the *Islah*. The soldiers did not make any statements of guilt and made no apologies stating that the Tanjung Priok incident was wrong. This position is obvious from the statement of General Try Sutrisno who, when he was asked whether signing the agreement meant pleading guilty, said: 'Our *Islah* with the Tanjung Priok people means mutual forgiveness. Do not talk about right and wrong. Mutual forgiveness is enough after we harbored enmity, suspicion and disagreement.' On another occasion he admitted that there was shooting in the incident by stating that 'the dead victims were buried soon and properly according to tradition, culture and

---

3. '*Meyjen (Purn) Pranowo Divonis Bebas*', *Suara Karya* 30 July 2004 at <www.suarakarya-online.com/news>.

4. Edy Can, '*AM fatwa: Islah Penyebab Para Saksi Tanjung Priok Cabut BAP*', *Tempo Interraktif*, 27 January 2004 at <http://www.tempointeraktif.com/hg/nasional/2004/01/27/brk,20040127-19,id.html>.

religion'. This statement clearly does not show any sense of guilt nor does it admit to legal accountability.

So what restores and heals the victims? What is the power of *Islah*? How can truth and moral judgment be neglected and yet restorative justice be achieved? I can see other components of restorative justice that played important roles in bringing a sense of justice to the victims who participated in the *Islah*. The first is the official acknowledgment of the harm done to the victims. While there was no moral judgment of the soldiers who were suspected of being the offenders, there was acknowledgment from them of the harm and pain of the victims caused by the incident. In this process both victims and offenders were accorded respect and concern. The *Islah* process also allowed dialogues between victims and offenders which empowered victims and encouraged offenders to be responsible. The empowerment of the victims came from the sympathy from the military and the recognition of their suffering. Though there was no explicit statement from the offenders of the admission of wrongdoing, affirmation of the suffering and a sense of responsibility for this were seen as forms of admission, even if not acceptance of total guilt.

The payment of restitution was also seen as a powerful indicator of the offenders' responsibility for the acts. Most of the victims or victims' families are poor. Besides being victims of the Tanjung Priok tragedy, they were also victims of an economic system based on injustice and the unequal distribution of resources. In this situation restitution proved helpful not only in the form of cash payment, but also as a means of reconciliation between victims and the offenders.

Another factor that empowered victims was their personal involvement in the *Islah* process. One aspect of the original crime was that it took all power from the victims, who were seeking to have their position heard. The victim's sense of self-determination was restored to them through their participation in the *Islah* process. For restorative justice to occur it is suggested that personal engagement is an important pillar in establishing victim confidence. The restoration process requires the participation of the primary parties, both victim and offender, in the decision-making process.[5]

Perhaps, the most influential factor in the process of *Islah* is that it has used the tools of religion to establish restorative solutions between some

---

5. Howard Zehr, *The Little Book of Restorative Justice* (Pennsylvania: Good Books, 2002), 24.

victims of the Tanjung Priok incident and military soldiers who were suspected of being perpetrators. I am not sure whether the facilitators of *Islah* specifically referred to Islamic religious sources. However, there is a definite religious power in this term, being an Arabic and Islamic term, and respected religious leaders facilitated the process. Tanjung Priok is a devout Muslim community and the victims of the Tanjung Priok incident were Muslims activists. A main characteristic of religious Indonesian people is their honour and respect for their religious leaders. Their near-total submission to their religious leaders gives these leaders a spiritual power to orient life for the establishment of happiness and satisfaction of the *jema'ah* (congregation). The concept of *Islah* itself is close to the concept of *sulh* in Islamic law. This is an important term in Islamic law (*shari'ah*), a form of contract (*'aqd*) between the individual and the community that is legally binding. According to Islamic law, the purpose of *sulh* 'is to end conflict and hostility among believers so that they may conduct their relationships in peace and amity'.[6] The spirit of *sulh* 'is derived from the *Qur'an* that prefers peace settlement to regulate the extent of punishment (*qisas*) and retribution with the principle of equity and enjoins forgiveness in cases of apology and "remission"'.[7] In this spirit the *Qur'an* says:

> O ye who believe! The law of equality is prescribed to you in case of murder. The free for the free, the slave for the slave, the woman for the woman. But if remission is made by the brother of the slain, then grant a reasonable demand, and compensate him with handsome gratitude. This is a concession and a mercy from your lord. (*Qur'an* 2:178)

> The recompense for injury is an injury equal thereto (in degree): but if a person forgives and makes reconciliation, his reward is due from Allah . . . But indeed if any show patience and forgive, that would truly be an affair of great solution. (*Qur'an* 42:40–3)

---

6. George E Irani and Nathan C Funk, *Ritual of Reconciliation: Arab and Islamic Perspectives* (Kroc Institute, 2000), 21. <http://www.nd.edu/~krocinst/ocpapers /op_19_2.pdf>

7. Irani and Funk, *Ritual of Reconciliation*, 26.

As the victims of the Tanjung Priok incident were Muslim activists who were demanding the application of Islamic law in Indonesian society, the *Islah* solution presented 'medicine' in the absence of Islamic law in Indonesia. Besides this, there had already been an unpromising and lengthy legal process, so both the victims and offenders were spiritually motivated to find an eternal solution before they died. As Muslims they believe that problems in human relationships should be resolved in this world to be accounted in the hereafter.

However, the practice of restorative justice is a process, in which there can be varying degrees of restoration: fully restorative, largely restorative, partially restorative and pseudo- or non-restorative.[8] I'd like to say that the outcome of the *Islah* process was largely restorative. However, while *Islah* works towards the healing of the victim and reconciliation with the offenders, there is a negative dimension to it. Because its focus is restitution, there is a lack of accountability with no attempt to uncover the full truth of the abuses and pass moral judgment on the perpetrators of these abuses. As there was no admission of guilt from the offenders, the peace agreement achieved through the *Islah* may allow them to ignore the wrongdoing they have committed. This would not prevent the offenders from repeating the wrongdoing in the future.

I think the victims' decision to go with the *Islah* process was mainly due to the absence of any real alternative options. The ideal solution may be uncovering the truth that would explain to them the reason for the pain they suffered and bring the perpetrators to justice. Without this, the wound of the victims can easily open up again in the future. Another problematic aspect of *Islah* is that it was not seen as a satisfactory conclusion for many other victims and communities.

Restoration with truth and moral judgment: the prospects of the Tribunal and the Truth and Reconciliation Commission in Indonesia

While those who were willing to participate in the *Islah* process decided not to see truth and moral judgment as essential elements, for most victims of the Tanjung Priok incident these are pivotal elements and thus they saw the *Islah* process as flawed and disappointing. They claimed that *Islah* was a trick by the military to protect its high-ranking members whom they believed to be involved in the incident. They believed that those victims who participated in *Islah* were pressured into doing so by the army. In fact, the victims who did not want to participate in *Islah* did not reject the concept. However, they

---

8.   Irani and Funk, *Ritual of Reconciliation*, 45.

argued that *Islah* must take place *after* the truth had been established. Am Fatwa, one of the victims who was not involved in *Islah*, said that he agreed with *Islah* but that it must first be established who was right and who was wrong. Therefore, *Islah* can work only after a due legal process. For him, it is admission of the wrongdoing which forms the sense of justice for the victims.[9]

The victims who are did not want to pursue *Islah* are still able to seek justice through the tribunal and TRC. The two options were legalised by the Indonesian Constitution (chapter 47; 26/2000). However, these are difficult processes that are still a long way from true justice. Experiences of truth and reconciliation commissions in many countries show that acknowledging the truth is not only difficult, but also dangerous. I imagine that the military would be defensive if asked to admit and take institutional responsibility for human rights violations in the past. As has been said, the military and the New Order people still have strong power today in the bureaucracy, the political and the business institutions. They will fight against any process using every power they have to save the old elites of the military and New Order. In a situation where they take offence they can still use the politics of terror. In this situation, tribunal justice seems unpromising and the victims become despairing. The release of soldiers who had been accused, in the case of the Tanjung Priok incident, is a clear example of the unpromising legal process.

Similarly, the TRC whose primary focus is on uncovering the truth made many people sceptical. Conflict of interests between the old elite still in the legislation process and the reformists makes the TRC, which has been proposed since 2000, impossible to carry out. There is a strong tendency for the military to manipulate the TRC to protect their soldiers. Many people see that the goal and *raison d'etre* of the TRC is amnesty instead of reconciliation. In the proposal of the TRC, it is mentioned that that TRC recommends amnesty to the violators of human rights regardless of whether or not they experience guilt and the desire for forgiveness.[10] Therefore, the development of the legislation process for the TRC in the DPR shows the tendency to change the name of the commission from 'Truth Commission and Reconciliation' to 'Commission of National Unity and Reconciliation'. It was reported that the military commission in the DPR demanded the removal of the term 'truth' in order to create national unity. The process of uncovering

---

9. Can, *'AM fatwa: Islah Penyebab Para Saksi Tanjung Priok Cabut BAP'*.
10. Budiarto Danujaya, *'Rekonsiliasi Menuju Indonesia Baru'*, *Kompas*, 16 December 2003.

the truth is seen as making the possibility of national unity unlikely. Djasri Marin, a senator from the military, said: 'Let's bury the past for the future'.[11]

Those who seek justice from the legal process and the TRC are taking a long and difficult path. Truth has become expensive. The experience of the TRC in South Africa, which was largely successful, showed that bargaining between the political interests of the old and new powers determined the success of the TRC. The situation in Indonesia is different from that in South Africa. The clear boundary between old and new power elements in South Africa made it easier to bargain towards reconciliation. But there is no such clear boundary between old and new political elements in Indonesia. It is still not easy to separate reformist and New Order powers in Indonesian politics today. There are also many parties and opportunists who are likely to stand in the middle between the reformist and New Order orientations. Additionally, the New Order still has a strong influence both in society and at a high political level. The TRC was proposed because of international pressure. However, in this situation, the military and the New Order powers were still able to manipulate it for their own particular interests.

In this situation, restoration for those who seek justice through the acknowledgement of truth must be seen as possible. The long process of finding justice can eventually give victims empowerment through self-determination. The intensity of this process and the openness of the political climate in contemporary Indonesia will give more chance to the victims, at least in bringing the case to public attention. This will be encouraging and empowering where the victims can get sympathy and recognition of their plight from the public, instead of from legal institutions. Stigmatisation of the victims and their families is one of the most serious effects of the New Order human rights violation. When the victims gain recognition and sympathy from public, they will also gain rehabilitation.

In the context of the focus on restoration, I think priority must be given to the reparation processes such as rehabilitation, restitution and compensation. The *Islah* process has shown restoration to victims through these three elements. Reparation becomes the primary right of the victims, while truth and justice, in term of punishment, become the secondary rights. As restorative justice suggests, focus is to be given to the harm and needs of the victims.

---

11.   Danujaya, 'Rekonsiliasi Menuju Indonesia Baru'.

6

Pleasure and Grief, in Violence

Jione Havea

Without the capacity to mourn, we lose that keener sense
of life we need in order to oppose violence.[1]

Speaking is impossible, but so too would be silence or
absence or a refusal to share one's sadness.[2]

As interpreters of holy scriptures—at homes, prisons, mosques, synagogues, churches, shrines and beyond—we can no longer step over the tremors and spills of violence in our sacred literatures, and in our contexts and interpretive practices.

Split a sacred text, violence is there.[3] Take the Judeo-Christian Bibles, for instance. From the garden story in *Genesis* to the longing for home in *2 Chronicles,* the last book in the Hebrew Bible, to the last warnings in *Revelation,* the final book in the Christian Bible, multiple manifestations of violence (physical, imagined, ideological, religious, cultural and so forth) hold up the structures of the Bible. The *Varna* system established by Hindu *Vedas,* which segregates society into four privileged castes plus the *Dalits*—formerly

---

This paper was originally given at a conference run by the United Theological College, North Parramatta, Sydney and will appear in a forthcoming ATF Press publication entitled *Validating Violence—Violating Faith?*, edited by William Emilsen and John Squires.

1. Judith Butler, *Precarious Life: Powers of Mourning and Violence* (New York: Verso, 2004), xviii–xix.
2. Jacques Derrida, *The Work of Mourning*, edited by Pascale-Anne Brault and Michael Naas (Chicago: University of Chicago Press, 2001), 72.
3. See *The Destructive Power of Religion*, edited by J Harold Ellens, four volumes (London: Praeger, 2004); Jack Nelson-Pallmeyer, *Is Religion Killing Us? Violence in the Bible and the Quran* (Harrisburg: Trinity, 2003); John D'Arcy May, *Transcendence and Violence: The Encounter of Buddhist, Christian, and Primal Traditions* (New York: Continuum, 2003).

known as the Untouchables, who are not included in the caste system—is also violating. Into this niche would fit the primarily degrading attitudes toward women in the sacred texts of the world's major religions,[4] including the vast and varied canon of Buddhist scriptures.

In our everyday life, violence is there too, in its many forms. From the racially loaded police chases at Redfern (NSW) to the faces of refugees turned away from first world borders, to the victims (crops, animals, humans, earth) of natural disasters, to the strike of machetes and the thunder of bullets and bombs (often waged under religious motivations), to the hidden beatings and verbal abuses in domestic spaces, violence is there. Insofar as location (concrete and ideological) and experience (personal and communal) steer our biblical interpretations and constructions, and in order for our interpretations to have public relevance, the escalation of violence in human societies demands our attention.[5] Violence is all around us, in biblical texts and on our paths.

Step back if you can from the act of interpretation, and you might be surprised to find manifestations of violence in what we do as interpreters. I have in mind here both the uprooting effect of the interpretive process— insofar as we analyse and unpack texts from different times and places so that they make sense in our placements—and the capacity of the interpretations that we produce to inspire violence. We often take refuge under the shadows of contextualisation, but we don't always account for the tears of relocation (to the text, and to the people and cultures from and through which the text has journeyed) that are required in order for contextualisation to happen. The interpretive task is a political task, many have argued, and interpreters often butt heads and cry, 'that's wrong' or 'that's silly' at each other's imagination and reconstruction. Those are also manifestations of violence, at a nonphysical level, I would argue.

Violence abounds, overflows and intermingles, around and in the act of interpretation. In light of the foregoing, how then may we, as interpreters, proceed? With caution, for sure, and being mindful of the web on which

---

4. See *Violence Against Women* (Maryknoll, New York: Orbis, 1994), edited by Elisabeth Schussler Fiorenza and M Shawn Copeland; Marie M Fortune, *Sexual Violence: The Sin Revisited* (Cleveland: Pilgrim, 2005); Aruna Gnanadason, *No Longer a Secret: The Church and Violence Against Women* (Geneva: World Council of Churches, 1993).

5. Of course, there are various ways and degrees in which *we may allow contexts to condition* our theological constructions and biblical interpretations!

violence tangles. In this chapter, I want to move beyond identifying and explaining the presence and the kinds of violence there are in the Bible,[6] toward *coming to terms with the web on which violence tangles* or, to use more Pacific Island images, *the mat on which violence sits* and *the sea that carries violence across*. My aim is to make violence understandable without making biblical violence—whether in the name of God and of God's chosen people or otherwise—acceptable. I propose to do this by sketching the *interrelation between violence, pleasure and grief*. But first, I shall briefly identify three of the currents in the sea of presuppositions that launch me unto this study.

Sea of presuppositions

First, I presume that sacred texts, from the West, East, and in-between, contain and disguise violence and so I feel that I do not need to argue or prove that there is violence in the Bible.[7] But for the ones who are in doubt, any children's storybook with pictures on brave young David defeating the giant, or Jesus hanging from the cross, should do the job. Artworks that are more graphic will also be helpful. The nineteenth-century illustrator of the Bible, Gustave Doré, has two illustrations of the Deluge that expose the senseless

---

6. See James G Williams, *The Bible, Violence and the Sacred: Liberation from the Myth of Sanctioned Violence* (San Francisco: Harper, 1992); *Sanctified Aggression: Legacies of Biblical and Postbiblical Vocabularies of Violence*, edited by Jonneke Bekkenkamp and Yvonne Sherwood (London: T&T Clark International, 2003); Phyllis Trible, *Texts of Terror: Literary-Feminist Readings of Biblical Narratives* (Philadelphia: Fortress, 1984); Renita J Weems, *Battered Love: Marriage, Sex and Violence in the Hebrew Prophets* (Minneapolis: Fortress, 1995); Cheryl Kirk-Duggan, *Pregnant Passion: Gender, Sex, and Violence in the Bible* (Atlanta: SBL, 2003); Cheryl B. Anderson, *Women, Ideology, and Violence: Critical Theory and the Construction of Gender in the Book of the Covenant and the Deuteronomic Law* (London: T&T Clark International, 2004); Matthes Shelly, *Violence in the New Testament* (New York: T&T Clark, 2005); Rene Girard, *Violence and the Sacred*, translated by Patrick Gregory (Baltimore: John Hopkins University, 1977); *Violence Renounced: Rene Girard, Biblical Studies, and Peacemaking*, edited by Willard M Swartley, (Telford, Pennsylvania: Pandora, 2000).
7. For a short reading see John J Collins, *Does the Bible Justify Violence?* (Minneapolis: Fortress, 2004).

violence in that story.[8] In one, the viewer is confronted with a naked couple, in water rising up to their groins, holding up a child onto a crowded rock, maybe the top of a mountain, on which sits a tiger with a cub in her mouth. In this work Doré portrays the child reaching down to the couple, as if s/he is about to fall off the safety of the rock. Paradoxically, safety for the falling child is on the side of a tiger with a cub. In the second image, bodies of humans and animals climb out from the water and Doré captures the tree breaking from the weight of the people, and as they fall back into the deadly water Doré draws the attention of the viewer to Noah's Ark floating at a distance. The plight of the victims of the deluge becomes more visible and more piercing because of the safety represented by the distant ark in the background. One can't help seeing violence in these images, violence often overlooked when one only reads the biblical text.

Interpreters are blinded to the presence of violence in the Bible for a variety of reasons, including the refusal to see the bloodiness in the *acts of God* for the sake of God. Such blinding attitudes of piety depart from the form of piety in the story of Job, the innocent sufferer who questioned God and debated with religious traditions, a critical attitude that can also be heard in the lamenting voices in the Psalter. In other words, to be blinded to the violence in the Bible is to shut up cries such as:

> My God, my God,
> why have you abandoned me;
> why so far from delivering me
> and from my anguished roaring?
> My God,
> I cry by day—You answer not;
> By night, and have no respite (Ps 22:2–3).

Second, I presuppose that violence in holy scriptures contributes to the violence that takes place in contemporary societies. In other words, I want to believe that holy scriptures do influence the way people live, and the way things are.[9] This presupposition would be difficult to defend in my current

---

8. One may view these images at *Biblical Art on the WWW* (<http://www.biblical-art.com/index.htm>) and *The Gustave Doré Art Collection* (<http://dore.artpassions. net/>).

9. See also Patricia M McDonald, *God and Violence: Biblical Resources for Living in a Small World* (Scottdale, Pennsylvania and Waterloo, Ontario: Herald, 2004).

location: when I moved to Australia in 2000, I was surprised with how eager my new friends and colleagues tried to convince me that Australia, compared to the United States, was a secular society. Why did they, mostly church folks, find it necessary to tell me that this was the case? Why did they assume that their perception of Australian societies is actually the way Australian societies are? What were they trying to say? What were they trying to hide? What did they gain by driving a wedge between the secular and the sacred? Were they hiding the influence of religion upon contemporary Australia? Were they disguising the place of religion in the settlement, or should I say invasion, of Australia? Were they telling me that my work is irrelevant because I deal with a religious text but their society is not religious? Does secularity equal un-religiousness? Were they simply reacting to the fact that I am Tongan, a native of a country of religious adherents whose population is almost all Christians? God forbid that a Tongan should teach, as I have been told, let alone teach anything about the Bible.

The irony is that the same people also told me that Australia is a multicultural society and, for six years now, I have been wondering if these friends say that Australia is secular *because* it is multicultural. Do they see Australia as secular because it is multicultural and multifaith? If so, then Australia must be secular because of its non-Christian people, even though non-Christians are people of other faiths. I stand to be corrected. And at this time, I also wish to say that if we come to terms with our religious biases, which are racially motivated, we might realise that multicultural Australia is a religious society. That would enable us to understand how multicultural and multifaith scriptures contribute to the violence in our contemporary society. Let me add also that I find the separation of the sacred from the secular most unhelpful and unrealistic.

Third, I presuppose that acts of violence in scriptures have to do with the exercise of and/or threats to one's power and honour. I see a link between violence and the exercise of power, and I suspect that subjects are more violent when their power and/or honour is challenged or threatened. The story of Elisha and the group of youths in 2 Kings 2 is an example of violence taking place when the honour of a bald prophet is threatened. In response, he calls forth two she-bears to mangle forty-two youths, for behaving as one would expect: it is not strange that a group of youths would make fun of older/bald men.[10] When power is threatened, violence escalates; this suggests

---

10. See my 'Boring Reading, Forgotten Readers,' *Uniting Church Studies* 10/2 (2004): 22–36.

that violent subjects are not stable or secure because, if they were secure with their shortfalls, and with themselves, they would not have responded with violence.

These presuppositions hover around the issues that I will now address.

Web of biblical violence

At this juncture, I seek to make sense of the structure in which violence is contained and promoted in and by the Bible. I do not intend to justify violence, biblical or otherwise, but to explore how we might come to terms with the place of violence in the Bible and in the name of God. And also, to set a platform for imagining why accounts of violence, or *texts of terror* as Trible calls them, were included and sanctified in the Bible.[11] Trible focused on texts of terror for women, but we must acknowledge that subjects who suffer acts of violence in the Bible have many faces—such as the poor, the foreigners, the strangers, the young, the disabled, the widowed, the orphaned and so forth.[12]

Let me come to the issue from another angle: who benefits as a consequence of texts of terror? For whose interests were texts of terror included in the memories preserved in the Bible? These questions go to show that scriptural texts are written with particular interests in mind. Scriptural texts have agenda—we cannot claim that biblical texts do not have ideologies, as if it is only in their interpretation and application that they become political and violent. If the Bible did not have ideologies and/or the power to construct ideologies, it would not have survived its journey over centuries across many cultures and locations. The Bible is like a hurricane that gathers and grows in strength as it crosses bodies of water and cultures; it is a power-book whose 'power' contributes to its appeal for abuse and violence.

The Bible is political and loaded, hence a potential tool and weapon of violence. By acknowledging that the Bible has particular vested interests, and realising that readers too are interested, we are urged to read against the grain of texts of terror. To read against the grain of texts of terror is an ethical responsibility. This is the gist of David Clines's call for 'reading from left to right'.[13] Since the two main languages used in the Hebrew Bible, Hebrew and

---

11. Trible, *Texts of Terror*.
12. We should acknowledge, also, that there are other kinds of texts in the Bible; the Bible is more than its texts of terror.
13. David JA Clines, 'The Ten Commandments, Reading from Left to Right', in *Words Remembered, Texts Renewed: Essays in Honour of John FA Sawyer*, edited

Aramaic, are written from right to left, to 'read from right to left' is to buy into the agenda of the text. But to 'read from left to right' is to read against the grain of the text; this metaphor materialises the call to read 'from the left' in the ideological plane. To read from left to right requires that one shifts ones sympathies, for instance, from Abel to Cain, from Sarai to Hagar, from Jacob to Esau, from Judah to Tamar and Dinah, from Moses and Aaron to Miriam, from Joshua to Rahab, from the Israelites to the Canaanites and the Egyptians, and so forth. The call to read from left to right, against the grain of the text, is therefore an ethical call. It is a call to read on behalf of subjects rejected from the favor of the biblical narrator.

To read from left to right is to undermine the violent agenda of the text, which is not an easy task because 'violence' is one strand woven with many others. I alluded to one of those strands earlier—namely, power and honour—and in the remainder of this chapter I will address the intersection between violence and pleasure, and violence and grief.

Violence and pleasure

There is something pleasurable and obsessive about violence.[14] Violence continues and develops because it gives some kind of pleasure to violent and violating subjects. There are several bridges under this link between violence and pleasure.

First, on a personal level, I am intrigued with the way some of my friends, especially current inmates and ex-convicts, talk with pleasure about their strings of crimes. They know that their crimes are violent, hurtful and wrong, but they recall with fondness the rush of excitement in their violent actions, which blinds them to their good conscience and makes them want to do more. Violence is addictive because it is pleasurable. These friends often speak of the itch to 'do one more job', so that they can feel the excitement again. This is not such a strange attitude, for one could easily argue that it is the same kind of bearing that set explorers and colonisers upon the high seas, and extreme-sportspeople on their course. There is a rush in doing edgy and dangerous activities; and acts of violence pop one's heart into one's throat. When one does not get the expected rush at one level one moves to the next, and thus violence develops and accelerates.

---

by Jon Davies, Graham Harvey and Wilfred GE Watson (Sheffield: Academic, 1995), 97–112.

14. Another might also argue that pleasure and obsessions ride on the shoulders of violence, but that is the subject for another occasion.

Second, in sporting events, it is not uncommon that fans get into fights and brawls, sparking violence in relation and response to those events. Boxing and wrestling, for instance, attract many fans, some of who react with violence, juiced by alcohol and the energy of the crowd of rowdy spectators. Sporting events survive because of the rivalry between fans. These fans see their sport as entertainment, rather than as contact sports with violence. Wrestling and boxing are violent but they attract many fans who also see those events as forms of entertainment. The captivating appeal of wrestling and boxing is that fans find them pleasurable, bringing violence and pleasure into the same ring.

Third, leading from the foregoing, is the irruption of *jouissance* which is how Jacques Lacan signifies the condition of bliss, arrival or fulfillment, which can be associated with sexual orgasm but also with the attainment of a desired object or condition (for example, arriving at a distant land for a voyager, or reaching the top of [to conquer!] a peak for a climber).[15] *Jouissance* (a French term meaning 'enjoyment') is not a purely pleasurable experience but arises through augmenting sensation to a point of discomfort (as in the sexual act—where the cry of passion is indistinguishable from the cry of pain; or as in running a race—which is at once exhausting and pleasurable). To yield to such activities and experiences, another might argue, is to give oneself to the allure of returning to the inorganic primal state that preceded life (so Freud)—as if it is a return to the beginning, which is close to death, bearing the marks of self-sacrifice, or the death-drive. *Jouissance*, on the other hand, is a desire to transcend the present condition of lack. It is not about regressing, but transcending, and transgressing, the current state of lack, which an Augustinian might characterise as a fallen state to which we are condemned. *Jouissance* is where enjoyment and agony overlap, penetration merges the cry of passion with the cry of pain, as one breaks through from, transcends, the trapping arms of the present condition of lack. In the light of the foregoing, *jouissance* represents the stage at which violence and pleasure interpenetrate.

While there was tension—encouraged by an evil spirit of Yahweh (*ruah yhwh ra'ah*),[16]—between King Saul and King David, two persons anointed to

---

15. See Jacques Lacan, *Ethics of Psychoanalysis, 1959–1960: The Seminar of Jacques Lacan*, edited by Jacques Alain-Miller, translated by Dennis Porter (New York: Norton, 1992).

16. The Massoretic Text of 1 Sam 18:10 and 1 Sam 19:9 is open for translation. Most translations follow the lead of 1 Sam 16:14 thus rendering these two verses as 'evil

occupy one throne, David had opportunities to kill Saul but he, showing signs of someone basking in *jouissance*, claimed to be extending respect and loyalty to Yahweh's anointed. In the cave where Saul went to relieve himself (Hebrew: 'cover his feet'), when David cut off the corner of Saul's cloak (1 Sam 24), and in the Wilderness of Ziph, when David took the spear and water jar from Saul's head as he was sleeping (1 Sam 26), David did not touch Yahweh's anointed. After both instances, David proclaimed at the hearing of Saul's men that they failed to protect their king but fortunately, he spared him in honour of Yahweh. These are moments of *jouissance,* where David glares in the faces of his enemies!

Fourth, I briefly turn to Job, the upright person who experienced gratuitous suffering because Yahweh and Satan agreed on a wager. Satan had just returned from going back and forth on earth and Yahweh asked him if he noticed how upright Job was. Yahweh's bragging about his devotee sets a cycle of tests into motion, resulting in the destruction of Job's family, for the sake of a wager. Was this (lousy) wager necessary?[17] What did it try to prove? That Job would worship God regardless of the consequences? That Satan may have failed to notice Job, the kind of person for whom he was supposed to be searching? Most readers would accept Yahweh's evaluation that Job was an upright man. In whose interest, therefore, was the wager and tests conducted? The acceleration of violence from the destruction of properties to the killing of children is narrated as if it were a game in which God did not want to accept the counter-challenge by Satan, a game that God initiated.

Violence and pleasure intersect and critics hesitate to touch the victimisation of Job. It is less problematic to speak of suffering, whether innocent or otherwise, rather than victimisation—hence suffering becomes the distraction from the violence in the story world—for to do so would expose an abusive God.[18] It is easier to read from the end of the story where Job gets a new family as if to say that his suffering was not for nothing and as if the new family can take the place, and erase the memory, of the one lost earlier. It is

---

spirit of/from Yhwh/Elohim' but they might also be translated as 'spirit of Yhwh/Elohim [is] evil upon Saul'. This alternative translation gives the impression that Yhwh/Elohim is, truly, a jealous god!

17. There are interesting parallels between God's wager with the Satan and the vow that Jephthah makes to God in Judges 10–11, the need for which is also questionable.

18. See David Penchansky, *The Betrayal of God: Ideological Conflict in Job* (Minneapolis: Westminster John Knox, 1991).

also easier to delight in the pleasurable aspects of the story and the wager, and of the debates between Job and his three friends, blinding critics to the violent aspects. To account for these, reading against the grain, might lead one to embrace the solution suggested by Job's wife, 'Curse God, and die!' This is not because death is preferred to suffering, as if Job should submit to the death-drive, but because God deserves cursing, even if this means death. Her willingness to approach death is the point of transgression at the foundation of *jouissance.*

A similar instance in the Hebrew Bible is the account of the plagues in Exodus, where a succession of plagues occurs as if they were the works of a malevolent and abusive god. Unlike the story of Job, the plagues have to do with a group of people (Israel) and it involves people from another culture (Egypt). At first, the more hardship the plagues bring upon Egypt the more difficult the oppression of Israel becomes. Egypt was not the only one plagued; Israel was violated as a consequence. Violence has many tentacles, grabbing more than one victim each time.

Whenever I read the account of the plagues in Egypt, I ask myself: when will the violence stop? When will Yahweh stop hardening Pharaoh's heart so that he may allow Israel to go? It feels as if Yahweh is just fooling around, pulling the strings and enjoying it also, at the expense of Egypt. The outcome is that, so to speak, the screws tighten harder and harder on Israel. According to this view, the violence that fell on Egypt and Israel was pleasurable to Yahweh and Pharaoh; this is the kind of pleasure that draws people to wrestling and boxing matches. Yahweh and Pharaoh were aware of the violence involved, but they were also pleased with the experience!

The pleasure in and of violence is absurd. And if we wish to untangle and overcome violence we need to both explore how violence and pleasure might be the affects of the same experience *and* expose the absurdity of that gory kind of pleasure. If we wish to read against the grain of texts of terror, we need also to name and challenge the forms of pleasure that fund them: in the story of Job, this pleasure is in the realisation that God is worshipped for nothing; in the plagues of Egypt, this pleasure is in the fear of the God of Israel.

Violence and grief
I grab in this section the line that Jacques Derrida and Judith Butler tow[19]: societies that have opportunities and rituals to address and express their grief

---

19. See especially Derrida, *The Work of Mourning*; Butler, *Precarious Life.*

and mourning are not too violent,[20] and if they are violent their violence is not extreme. Those societies have channels through which they embrace and unload their pain. Mourning becomes a way of giving relief to grief before it irrupts in one's face in various forms of violence. Moreover, when in response to the departure or passing of another, mourning is a way of continuing to be connected, to be in touch with, to speak to, the other who has departed or passed, even though the other is gone, and precisely because that other is gone. Mourning is an opportunity to break through the limits of life, to reach beyond to the one who has departed. On the other hand, societies that discourage mourning also bar the embrace and expression of their grief, and this often bubbles to the point where they burst into extreme forms of violence. Both of these attitudes, the expression and the suppression of grief, are evident in the Bible.

First of all, regarding the expression of grief, voices of lamentation in the Psalter and beyond are windows for people to express their grief and sense of despair:

> How long, O Lord, shall I cry out
> And You not listen,
> Shall I shout to You, 'Violence!'
> And You not save? (Hab 1:2, JPS)

Voices of lamentation break through the barrier between humans and their God, calling the latter into accountability. Unfortunately, some of the voices of lamentation call for extreme actions:

> Fair Babylon, you predator,
> a blessing on him who repays you in kind
> what you have inflicted on us;
> a blessing on him who seizes your babies
> and dashes them against the rocks! (Ps 137:8–9, JPS)

---

20. I do not limit grief and mourning to the responses given to the death of another human. I see grief and mourning in responses to other losses in life also, such as departure (to another land) and abuse (in which case one loses 'face' through verbal, psychological and physical insult). Grief and mourning are the stuff of relationality, so they may not be as evident or as valued in cultures of individualism.

One of the challenges therefore is how to confine such severe drives to the realms of grief and mourning so that they do not break through into violent actions. Biblical rules and regulations operate in this groove: in principle, rules and regulations bring into words actions and behaviors that are destructive so if people are mindful of these they can transfer their pain through the laws. When we read laws, unfortunately, we are easily bored and feel restricted, and rightly so. But laws can be openings for unloading one's pain (especially for complainants and the abused, who need to unload pain the most; ironically, to feel being restricted by the laws is to reveal where one stands and one's privileges—in other words, laws are restrictive to people with privileges). The sacrificial system operates along the same line: it provides opportunities for worshippers to channel and transfer their guilt and grief to the sacrificed elements.[21]

Secondly, regarding the suppression of grief, I consider the outbreaks of violence as the consequence of suppressed grief. When the Levite, back at his home, dismembered his concubine then sent a limb to each of the tribes of Israel—after having gone to woo her back and ending up spending extra nights with his persistent father-in-law, then being diverted on the way home—I wonder if his action was the bursting of grief (Judg 19). He went to bring back his wife, and returned with the body of a fallen woman. We can't determine from the text if she was already dead when he picked her up and placed her on his donkey,[22] so we can't be sure if she was dead or alive when he dismembered her, or when she died, but his excessive behaviour suggests a bitter and grieving soul. He was bitter and grieving because of his failure in his mission, because he did not return with what he set out to gain, and because of the appalling state of his concubine's body when he reached home. Between Gibeah and home, his bitterness and grief boiled, and then burst upon arrival. If his bloody violent behavior is due to excessive bitterness and grieving, then I can understand it, even though I do not accept it.

The story of Absalom contains another example of the bursting of grief. Amnon, his half-brother, raped Tamar, Absalom's full-sister, and when Absalom heard about it, he suppressed his grief and Tamar's pain and wailing saying: 'Was it your brother Amnon who did this to you? For the present,

---

21. There are other effects of the legal and sacrificial systems, and the violent and rigid implications of the sacrificial system are absurd, but those are subjects for another place!

22. See Mieke Bal, 'A Body of Writing', in *A Feminist Companion to Judges*, edited by Athalya Brenner (Sheffield: Sheffield Academic Press, 1993), 208–30.

sister, keep quiet about it; he is your brother. Don't brood over the matter (2 Sam 13:20).'[23] How can a raped victim, or any other victim, *not* brood over the violence committed? To do what Absalom suggests requires the suppression of a lot of grief. Two years later, excessive violence broke through. Absalom urged his father, who did not accept his invitation, to send Amnon and the other princes to the shearing of his flocks. Absalom organised a party for his brothers, and ordered his attendants to strike and kill Amnon when they see that he is merry with wine. This brought the feud between Absalom and David to a boil, leading to open rebellion, to Absalom laying with his father's concubines 'before the eyes of all Israel (2 Sam 16:22) ', and eventually to the hanging death of Absalom at the hands of David's men (see 2 Sam 13:1–19:1). There are probably other (personal and political) reasons why Absalom killed Amnon, but what draws me to this story in this reading are the violent upshots of the suppression of grief.

I highlighted in this section the links between violence and grief, in life and in religious texts, and suggest that if we want to uproot violence we must also deal with the grief that gave birth to it *as well as* the grief it causes. There is an interesting example of this in Exodus 22:21–23:

> You shall not ill-treat any widow or orphan. If you do mistreat them, I will heed their outcry as soon as they cry out to Me, and My anger shall blaze forth and I will put you to the sword, and your own wives shall become widows and your children orphans. (JPS)

On the surface, this law protects the widow and orphan, who has already suffered the grief of having lost a husband or parent. But this law has potential to bring about more grief, for the one who breaks it shall be killed and his wives will become widows and his children will be orphans. Grief feeds violence. Violence feeds grief.

---

23. There are other places in the Bible where grief and mourning are discouraged. One way of reading Jesus' comment 'let the dead bury their dead' (Mt 8:22) is to say that Jesus was moving the living away from the dead. Jesus, however, from familial and communal points of view, is insulting to the dead and the departed. Similarly, is the instance when Jesus refuses to receive a visit from his family but responds that his mother and siblings are those that do the will of his father (Mt 12, Mk 3, Lk 8). These comments are insulting especially since Jesus announced them in the hearing of the public.

In extreme cases such as these, as suggested earlier, one of our challenges is to name, express and contain grief so that excessive violence does not happen. This chapter, if it is not evident yet, has attempted to show that *sacred texts, and their interpretations, play a role in the suppression, expression and restitution of violence.*

Violence does not sit alone

Imagine, if you may, violence as a disfiguring body sitting on a mat, and imagine that we want to throw this body off.[24] That will of course involve energy and skill, and our action will be seen as an expression of violence!

Nonetheless, continue imagining: as we approach the mat, we see other bodies sitting alongside, in conversation with, joyfully and irritatingly, laughing and crying with, and against, violence; they have formed a circle, and bonded relationships, so to throw one of them out requires that we face those other bodies.[25] I identified some of these bodies above: sacred texts, interpreters, power, status, gender, security, ritual, religion, pleasure and grief. There are other bodies I have not taken into account, such as the physical body (who is human? what constitutes life?), the matter of relationality (who is? who belongs?), the issue of cruelty (what gives? what violates?), and so forth.

Imagine then, as we reach down to grab violence in order to throw it out, we hear the other bodies saying, in fact, crying out, 'Wait. Sit. Talk to us first!'

---

24. See also *Nurturing Peace: Theological Reflections on Overcoming Violence*, edited by Deenabandhu Manchala (Geneva: World Council of Churches, 2005).

25. As practitioners of intertextuality and transtextuality affirm, no text sits alone so the sea of texts and stories needs to be addressed in their intertwining structures.

Contributors

Mohammad Iqbal Ahnaf has a Master's degree from the Centre for Justice and Peacebuilding, Eastern Mennonite University, Harrisonburg, USA. He is currently a junior faculty member at Gadjah Mada University, Yogyakarta, Indonesia in the Centre for Religious and Cross-cultural Studies where he co-facilitates a course on religion, violence and reconciliation. Author of *The Image of the Other as Enemy: Radical Discourse in Indonesia* (2006), he is Indonesia's representative to the Media Initiative Program of the Asian Muslim Action Network and manages *Amana Quarterly*, a magazine concerned with interfaith and peacebuilding in Asia.

Kathy Galloway, an ordained minister, author of many books, lecturer and consultant, is leader of the Iona Community, an ecumenical Christian community based in Scotland seeking new ways of living the gospel. The focus of her work is social justice issues, especially those relating to people living in poverty and issues concerning women. As a feminist and liberation theologian, she is committed to a praxis methodology, doing theology with those who are at the margins.

James Haire, a Uniting Church minister, is Professor of Theology at Charles Sturt University, Canberra, Executive Director of the Australian Centre for Christianity and Culture and Director of the Public and Contextual Theology Strategic Research Centre. He was formerly President of the National Council of Churches in Australia and the Uniting Church in Australia. He is on the board of four international theological journals.

Jione Havea, a native of Tonga and ordained by the Methodist Church of Tonga, now teaches Old Testament studies at the United Theological College in Sydney, focusing on literary and cultural interpretation and human relationships.

Jonathan Inkpin is General Secretary of the New South Wales Ecumenical Council. Between 2002–4 he worked as national coordinator of the Decade to Overcome Violence for the National Council of Churches in Australia.

Patrick J McInerney is a Columban Missionary and member of the Columban Centre for Christian-Muslim relations in Sydney. He lectures in Inter-religious Dialogue at the Catholic Institute of Sydney.